The Man Who Walked the Dog

The D.J. Superior/DMX Story

Written By:

Jerome Enders

Published by:

Tut Publishing

Front and back cover by D.K.

Printed in the United States of America

ISBN: 978-0-578-09008-5

TABLE OF CONTENTS

FOREWORD

In 1997 the world was blessed with the first DMX album "It's Dark as Hell and Hell is Hot." It automatically shot to the top of the billboard charts and in record sales. Then shortly after within a year's period of time DMX released his second album "Flesh of my Flesh, Blood of my Blood," and again music lovers around the world went to the stores and into their wallets, pocketbooks, and made the album go multi- platinum breaking long standing record sales. It also helped to propel this artist to the top of the music industry, and entertainment world.

In the world of entertainment there is a saying that is often quoted and it says that "everything is in the timing." It was obvious that the stars aligned and opened up a gate way and when DMX walked through the porthole, his music hit the four corners of the earth. He introduced the world to another chamber of hip-hop and set the bar for artists for generations to come.

How was this man able to come on the scene and fill a void that the death of Tupac and Biggie left?

He quickly moved into the big screen making block buster movies. Then the dark side kicks in and he is now getting arrested and making headlines across the world. I was thinking, "Y'all must have forgotten the fact that before DMX got on the music scene, he was getting arrested and he told you what he was about in his first album." I know everyone thought it was just a song. The fact is that DMX put his life into songs and it is strongly argued that is the very reason the world fell in love with him; because he was real and true to himself and it reflected in his music. You could just feel it!

An inquisitive person will ask the question "Who are you?"

I'm the guy that Smokey Fontaine the author of DMX's autobiography E.A.R.L was told to see in order for him to give his book a stronger foundation and more credibility.

Who am I?

I'm the guy that whenVH1 was making the documentary; DMX behind the music had to come and see to get the rare classics behind the scene video footage of DMX to share with the world; as well as to make the documentary more credible. I'm the guy who had the dog in the kennel located at 57 Mulford Gardens apartment 2-B, and that's where I fed him the formula. That's where we trained. The training regimen was so intense. I was able to capture hours and hours of rare unreleased recordings and video footage that are sought after by DMX fans around the globe. This book is written in response to the many emails I have been receiving from home and abroad such as Australia, Europe, Africa, and Japan don't forget DMX has a worldwide fan base and has gone on several world tours. With that in mind I began to notice that people from different parts of the world connect to something I helped build and played a major part in.

Some argue the fact that if DMX didn't have a drug problem he would have gone down as one of the greatest of all time.

My response to them is Elvis had a drug problem and they call him the king, and the beetles had a serious drug problem but the fact remains that they have gone down in history as one of the greatest bands ever. There are hundreds of books written about them, and the sad thing about it is that most of the authors of those books have never had actual dealings with these individuals. Their books are based on research and other people's experiences. However, my case is different because I was there I have first-hand experience. This book is also written with the intention to carry on the legacy of a talented man whose heart and reputation has been tarnished. However, by him having a strong work ethic produced enough material that could circulate for the next 10 to 15 years, and was so advanced in his craft that what he recorded in the mid 90's has more substance than most of the music that is out now-a-days.

Plus, I have a story to tell. Yeah, I walked the dog and in 1997 when he ran loose he bit a lot of people. He wagged his tail at a few people and even let some people pet him, **but he shitted on me**!

INTERLUDE

Some characters in history are just myths and then you have some figures in history where their stories are more factual.

Real legends their stories tend to be told throughout the ages. Well, in the mid 90's in the dirty mean streets of Yonkers, NY there was a Dog. The walker calls him "The Grand Champ" roaming the city streets looking for prey just before the setting of the sun. You would see packs of birds flying quickly with continued wind blowing, creating a whistle in the air as the streets begin to clear; the sun sets and an airy quietness blankets the city.

The 9-5 is over and with the nightlife comes a whole other cast of characters with rules and laws that govern the underworld. But one thing you could count on was that somewhere in the city someone was going to get a visit from a guy dressed in all black with a hoodie and some Tims on. Nine times out of ten, he will be accompanied by a partner. A red nose pit-bull named Boomer. The word on the streets was when approached by the duo, it was best to cooperate! With that being said, thousands of dollars of cash, jewelry, and drugs were taken as the duo escaped running away into the moonlight. Known to just a few at the time is that the dogs would return to the Kennel located at 57 Mulford Gardens some hours later. At that time, the dog called the grand champ had unusual talent in which he would write lyrics and songs all night until the break of dawn literally, and record several songs daily for months at a time; the legend has it years at a time. Meanwhile at the kennel, the dog was being nurtured, cared for, and fed. Whereas the other dog owners saw this dog as just being a stray, or a wild animal, DJ Superior just gave this dog a home.

Due to the circumstances associated with this particular dog, he had to have special care. In a city where there were a variety of other animals such as felines- cool cats, alley cats, cougars, and scaredy-cats; those in the bird family such as chicken heads and wings;

we also have your snakes- cobras, lizards and different breeds of the reptilian family; Those in the monkey family such as the baboon, gorillas, chimpanzee (intelligent monkey), and orangutans (the silly monkey's); Plus, a variety of other dogs such as Dobermans, poodles, plenty of mutts, and let's not forget the bitches! This particular dog was taken to the side and given special care and breeding because of his special bloodline. Eventually others that like to showcase dogs found an interest in this dog and came looking for him. The walker knew that this particular dog had to be handled with special care and even then, he was capable of anything.

One day there was a showcase of the top dogs and it was at that moment all of the other owners knew this dog was the one. Immediately some owners wanted to breed with this dog, and a few even tried to steal the dog from the walker in the midst of all the chaos. Sometimes the dog would escape but always found its way back home. One day the caretaker decided that the dog was growing up and that it was best to find a new caretaker, a new home for the "Grand Champ." But as the papers were about to be signed over to the new caretakers, the dog got loose and never returned.

As I have flashbacks of my experiences with him in the past, and my position in the present, and living in the now I realize that I was blessed with the curse. Out of all of the people in the world I was the chosen one to "Walk the Dog."

SCHOOL 12

I got the job at School 12 by starting off as a member of the Board of Directors. I started off as a young boss. Around me at that time were Soke Papasan Canty, Ken Jenkins, Clayton Lebouef, now Senator Andrea Cousins, the late Mayor Zaleski, Symra Brandon, and a few others that I can't recall at this time. I was grand-mothered in by a lady by the name of Julie Wilson who used her influence to get me into that position.

All of the other members of the board were older, well learned, and power brokers. I was in a rare privileged position in upper management at a young age. Many would have loved to be in my shoes. When I was younger I didn't realize what I had. Yeah, I lied about my age. I was only 16 or 17 at the time, but I told them I was 20 and they knew I wasn't.

When I was first introduced to Julie Wilson she thought I was a drug dealer. I don't know why she would think something like that. I guess it was the image I was giving off. She quickly realized that when she sat down to talk with me I had graduated from high school, I had completed two years in cooking school, and I had some goals set for myself. Later on she told me that she felt bad because she had prejudged me. As we continued to build our relationship she gave me wisdom and protection. She was a kind, good hearted Caucasian lady who happened to be married to a black man. Her connections helped me to get voted onto the Board.

Being a Board Member I was partly responsible for overseeing the functions of the facility and the allocation of funds. I found out very quickly that people were playing games especially with the money. I was asking questions that they didn't want me to ask. I had many questions about the money, and where it was being spent. The next thing I knew after four years on the Board I was given an office downstairs out of the way. I was still on the Board, but you can believe that they created some distance. Eventually after Julie died they offered me a job.

SUPERIOR & YOUTH AT SCHOOL 12

Here is a glimpse of what the other Board Members did to me. As soon as Julie passed away they took me off the Board and gave me a part time job. That was incredible to me because I went from being a prestigious Board Member to being demoted to a part time worker. I guess they did that to shut me up.

There are many institutions in society that are designed with the intentions of helping, but only a small percentage actually help. As I learned from Julie a lot of times people will say that we need more black people in positions of power. However, if you get the wrong black person in position they may do the same to you that a clansman would do or worse. I worked at School 12 from 1991 and it's currently 2009, and that is the only other job I have had besides working with the former Yonkers Mayor Zaleski.

Yonkers has a rich and long hip-hop history, and School 12 played a major role in that history. I realized the power position that I was in and with my music background I can make things happen. Therefore, I devised a plan that Julie, and myself began to implement it before she died. I told her that I knew someone who was going to become a star; and I needed her help with the parties not just at School 12, but throughout Westchester County. I brought the Wu-Tang Clan up to Yonkers and that speaks volumes by itself. I met the RZA downtown and we kicked it, he did a show for me for a minimal charge of $5,000 they came to Yonkers and blessed the town. That's when the song "Check your Neck" was out with Method Man, Old Dirty Bastard (O.D.B), the whole clan came that was a powerful day.

JULIE WILSON

Julie's motivation was to get the youth off the streets. She was truly amazed with me, I remember telling her that the streets are filled with amazing youth; but you will never get to know them if you don't get into their lives. She liked what I was doing, which is why she set up shop to keep the ball rolling. She helped set up my foundation. I also had a strong support with two other youth advocates named Leon Thomas & Irma Crews.

I learned a lot from the mentors that were there and are still there at School 12 to this day. Ms. Crews is there for the youth who don't have any father's in their life or active mother's. At the time School 12 was a supplement, and it became a parent for many children in the neighborhood.

KASUN & CREW

At the time I met X, Kasun was his DJ, but he was going around town robbing people. I was introducing X to a way of making money without sticking people up. I told him we can set up some parties and battles and make some good honest money. In the beginning he said that he didn't want to hear that shit! Then, we started to work it. Eventually Kasun got locked up and I had to carry on the torch.

I was always a DJ and did parties. I have over 600 flyers from parties that I have done with my name on them. Nobody can say that X made me, he didn't make me. He helped to expose my name, and I did the same for him. We had a group by the name of Gangsters of the Ghetto "G.O.G" with members Jinx, Assassin, JLA, and BM. The only competition in the streets was Bill Blass' crew "The Get Paid Staff," and "The Bomb Squad," which was the LOX, and of course Raw Rome but he was more of a dolo artist.

One of the things that I remember about School 12 that touched me was the ability to give troubled youth a place to go and relax and get their minds together. Many people that never really got along with each other in the streets or in school went there; they interacted in peace, and were brought together in unity. There were many nights people wanted to fight and do other foolish things, that is why I would have them sit there all day in the program and believe it or not you can get a lot done when you bring people together. Many of the guys didn't want to fight and do most of the crazy things they did. We provided a place that stimulated their idle minds and taught some social skills. I learned early that if you bring people together you can get more out of them, and in return they will respect you. Examine the history of School 12, the only serious problem they had was with the parties at night. During the day time when the building was filled with youth there were no serious issues. That's why we must continue to express ourselves because the media doesn't report success stories they are programmed that way. The media's job is to promote the negative images, and degradation of the inner city youth. The only time that you will hear about someone like me is when I'm getting arrested or something else along those lines. Or when I die everyone who knows me will have something good to say, and will reminisce and tell wonderful stories. Some will even have my picture with R.I.P. on their t-shirt saying that's my nigger. You can screw your face up with what I just said and how I said it, but that's how it is!

As in the case of Raw Rome if he didn't start writing they never would have paid homage to his contributions in the Yonkers Hip-Hop game. They wouldn't remember him. They would have said Raw Rome who? Or would have said yeah, yeah, yeah, he used to spit back in the days, and that would be it. School 12, Brown Eyes, Jam-N, Arthur's were all landmarks that were owned or ran by black people. The powers that be were merciful at that time. Do you think it was a coincidence that all of those social clubs died out slowly but surely? That was no coincidence somebody did that. People had a hand in that it was about money and control. Think about it.

As for the situation that happened to my home-boy Malachi in front of School 12 that terrible night when he was stabbed it made the news. As usual they blew it out of proportion tying School 12 and violence in together; Hip-Hop and violence and they were coming for my head. They needed someone to blame it on and a situation such as that I become the scapegoat. Here is the bottom line when Malachi was stabbed in front of School 12 that night it wasn't even his beef. He had nothing to do with it he went outside to break up what was going on. A dude from Mount Vernon was upset because he was unable to get inside the party to hurt someone. So he went across the street with his homees. Malachi followed him across the street and said to them

"Yo man you need to chill out and calm down that's my man in there and we all are cool. It's Bully's birthday and we're just trying to get our party on." The dude from Mt. Vernon said "Well if that's your man hold this for him" and stabbed him. Just like that. So the free party I put on for the hood turned into a blood bath. I was promoting Bully really hard back then and I was giving back to the hood that day. I decided to do a free party, which at the time was the best thing to do. What's funny is that people in the party were saying Bully is whack we don't fuck with him, but marketing shows me differently. I learned that eventually people that didn't feel an artist at one time or another would eventually come around once they continued going to parties and other promotional events. They would eventually find something that they liked about the artist. These are one of the little tricks I learned over the years to get an artist out there.

On top of the whole Malachi disaster the agency didn't want to back me up. They threw me to the sharks, but the streets backed me because they told what really happened. Malachi's mother informed those who needed to know what his reasons were for being at School 12 and mentioned that I had nothing to do with the violence that took place that night and the unfortunate death of her son. You may ask why they tried to throw me under the bus. I did parties there for years with the backing of the organization; however, when somebody died all of a sudden there's no more permission to do any parties. They couldn't find a contract for that night, you know the usual bullshit. When his mother stepped up and spoke out on my behalf everyone started apologizing and brown nosing me. A minute ago when they were protecting themselves from liability I was the fall guy. They had me in the newspaper with their media sensationalism. I started pulling strings and speaking to some people and that's when the apologies came pouring out in another article. However, you know the article was really small. Apologies for people who are falsely accused are always small…only in America!

Another role model that I had been Papasan Canty he was very influential in my development. He gave me a better overstanding of the police and made me realize that all of them are not on the take.

Years ago I had a bad experience with the cops that left a bad taste in my mouth. I was on some…fuck the police shit! Sometimes cops are put in a position where they have to behave a certain way, or do certain things to appease the powers that be. You have to overstand some of the policies that the police have can lead to misconduct and corruption for example meeting quotas. Without crime there would be no police. Some officers keep nonsense going. The quotas help the budget; that equals money to pay officers. When you think about it they need you to be violent, reckless, and anti-social if not they wouldn't have their job. The two work hand in hand and with the ignorance on the rise they're going to have plenty of job security. So, Papasan taught me to develop relationships with a few cops that I could relate to and it would help my situation tremendously. They would have a chance to see what type of person I am, and what was going on in the building with the kids.

Overall listening to Papasan and getting to know the cops improved things for me. As time went on the police stopped bothering me. They would let me go while everyone else would still be against the wall, or in the car going downtown to Alexander Street.

That created another situation and I found I couldn't win for losing. This was all a learning experience. I went through four bosses at School 12 my current boss was from the Bronx, but I don't think she is familiar with the hood and the dynamics of it. If she is familiar it would reflect in her mentality and into the way she runs the community center. For example a kid that turns 21 or 22 years of age they are just swept under the rug and the door is closed on them. They were raised by us and continue to need our support. However, now we aren't or can't do anything for them all of the concentration is on the younger generation 18 and younger. She needs to see that you can't do that just as they reach that age. That age doesn't mean that they are mature or mentally developed them still need our guidance? They wanted me to just turn these young adults to the streets, but my conscience wouldn't allow me to do it, which they couldn't overstand.

STUDIO AT SCHOOL 12

I built a studio in School 12 using funded money, but when she got mad at me she tore down the studio just to aggravate and piss me off.

What type of leader is that?

I was building a studio at School 12 so that I could teach the youth that you can be just as important behind the scenes as on the stage. A lot of people don't know that fact that's why everyone wants to be the star. I would let them know that you can be behind the scenes and make more money than the person on the stage. Their reason for tearing down the studio was that it didn't meet fire department safety codes. They said that the panels I had up were flammable.

If that were the case why couldn't we just replace the panels? Why did they have to destroy the whole studio project?

For some reason the new administration did not like me. They were trying to find dirt on me, and they had people spying on me it was crazy! They would try to set me up. I don't drink but I would go into my office and there would be beer bottles in my garbage. Then, out of the blue they would want to investigate my garbage. Everyone knows that there is no drinking in the building. It's crazy but since 2005 they have been trying to rub me out and get rid of me. This lady is not an effective leader in my eyes, and leadership starts at the top. If your staff is not behind you then what do you have? Even when she tries to turn other staff against me that creates friction in the organization because they don't agree with her agenda against me. To top it all off they have informed me of her moves against me. My colleagues question her motives. I think she is very crafty and calculating.

Those who are wise amongst the staff acknowledge the fact that less concentration should be on me because the youth program is diminishing...quickly! The quality of care is changing and I am truly worried because I have seen other community centers fall because of elements of that nature. However, I'm studying the art of war right now and I see how they are coming at me. They are trying to assassinate my character and take away my resources hoping people will stop dealing with me. If I'm looked at as weak minded I will possibly feel not wanted and just quit. That's an old trick.

Anyone that begins to ask the right questions becomes a threat and the questions I was asking was about budgeted money, budget sheets, etc. I don't know if she knew that I sat on the Board before she even thought about coming to Yonkers. I know about the organization from top to bottom. I didn't find anything wrong with my questions because I was looking for money for my program and from experience I know how the funds are allocated. All I wanted was to keep my kids off the streets. Fortunately for me I could go next door to the pizza shop and talk to Nile if I had to blow some steam off and get some knowledge. Also, Nile would feed the children in the neighborhood. Over the years he donated a lot of pizza he fed a lot of kids out of the goodness of his heart. I didn't always have to come out of my pocket and that was a blessing. To this day he says if I ever need anything just ask him.

For the last 10 years or so he never said no to me when I asked him for something. He cared for the people in the community. Through his love he taught me love; he's not even from the United States he is from Turkey. He was giving me more help than a so-called American would give. You know the one that loves apple pie and baseball and all of that stuff, but really don't have love for their fellow man. People are seeing through all of that lip service and fluff. Love is what Love does.

He showed love to the children at School 12, and to the projects at the Mulford reunions. The Chinese store wouldn't do it **(blood suckers of the poor)**, the sneaker store never did it **(blood suckers of the poor)**, and the liquor store never did it. The liquor store just raped the hood for the resources and talked to us disrespectfully. None of the merchants on Ashburton would kick back anything, which is why "Ashburton Pizza" gets love from the streets.

Tip for the Future Youth Advocates: ***Find and build a relationship with a connection in food. Remember to always incorporate food into your budget. Feeding people will take you a long way.***

I wish I was able to find some resources to help 20 year olds because they need attention. They need life skills and guidance. Some of them their minds are still young and immature. We turn them loose on society unprepared and inexperienced and expect them to survive.

Many times you have to put your money where your mouth is. We taught fitness one time at the center and I purchased the weights and pool table myself. I was so involved in the program. It was as though I was working for free because I was only being paid $25,000 a year. I was paid bi-weekly and was only taking home $687 after taxes. I was being exploited by my employers. Their goal was to get as much as possible from an employee and pay them as less as they can.

No matter which way I turned or to whom I reached out to I was being used or pimped, and this was not coming from the hands of a white man. When I was young I heard a lot of rhetoric about the suppressors of the black community; but it wasn't until I was older that I realized that almost everyone was involved in the exploitation and capitalization on the ignorance of poor people in my community.

A conversation with Papasan Canty:

Papasan Canty is a community activist, hall of fame martial artist, instructor, creator of the Kuroshi-Do (the way of the black warrior) style of karate. It is a style created by him and two others for inner city youth.

How did you become involved in martial arts?

I have been involved in martial arts since 1955. At that time I was introduced to judo and jujitsu by my uncle Marion Wallace who was a housing police officer in New York City.

When I was young growing up in Brownsville, Brooklyn I was getting into fights regularly coming home from school. He figured if I didn't learn how to fight that eventually I would have bigger problems; such as being jumped and getting hurt really badly, or being put in a position to defend myself in a really bad situation.

After about a summer of martial arts I fell in love with the art and continued to study Judo and Jujitsu. Later I got into boxing, and then karate in 1967. I went into the military and eventually was stationed in Japan and that became my turning point in martial arts. I got a chance to train with some of the masters while I was over there.

What did you learn while you were over there?

Well the first thing that I learned was that I was in good shape. This was back in the 60's and karate had just begun to hit the United States, and because I was already involved in karate under Sen-Se Bill Greene I was ahead of everyone else over there. (For more info. read help the Bear a Road Map to Grand Mastery by Soke Papasan Canty).

I became involved with the youth when I was discharged from the military in 1971; I began working at the Howard Houses Police Athletic League. At the time I was boxing, and then I became a counselor, and then the martial arts instructor, and lastly the assistant director. In 1980 I moved to Yonkers and started working in the Yonkers Community Action Program (YCAP) with Julie Wilson and Pat Sadler as their martial arts instructor and branched out from there.

In 1985 I became a Yonkers police officer and I tried to be an officer that builds his reputation on not the amount of children I lock up, but the amount that I can help. Through the many programs I had in town I worked with the youth division of the police department, which was right up my alley. I was a true community police officer. I worked on and off duty to get the job done.

What was your experience at School 12?

I started my dojo at School 12 to help the kids in the neighborhood mainly from the projects: School Street, Mulford Gardens, Cottage, and Scholbum (Slow Bomb), I had them all. Those kids trained with me and became so good I started taking them around the country and other countries; we went to Canada, Trinidad, and Puerto Rico. I started to build a good name for myself and Julie and Pat were pleased and just kept moving forward.

One of the kids that came out of the program was Mike Superior who was a rough edged kid who came up in the program. However, as an advocate in the program they were always trying to get him out of the program because he couldn't keep quiet. So, I began to teach him how to navigate in the system. From my dojo at School 12 I have taught at least three or four generations martial arts and that was one of the best kept secrets. Due to everything that was taking place in the hood most people would drive by and not know what we were doing. But, we were changing lives one student at a time.

I was once the President and C.E.O. of Y.C.A.P. and Superior was always on the Executive Board as a voice for the youth. I will say for the record that things wouldn't have happened in the building if it wasn't for him. Superior introduced a lot of the programs we had, we even had a studio in the building. Out of all of the years that I was there no one else ever had the thought of having a studio. That studio was the brainchild of Mike Superior under the guidance of some of his mentors such as: Julie Wilson, and Clayton Lebouef. Superior deserves a lot of credit, but he probably will not get it because they brought in people from out of town that don't know the history. Superior has been on the Board longer than anyone in the history of that building.

It was Papasan who also played a major role in helping DMX at a pivotal point early in DMX's career.

I say that Papasan was instrumental in helping DMX because it was Papasan who kept DMX out of jail long enough so that he could go on a major promotional tour early in his career. If DMX would have gone to jail at that time who knows how it would have affected history.

Papasan: I really wish that DMX would have reached back and pulled up Bill Blass with him I think that would have been another star that Yonkers would have produced. At this time DMX and Bill Blass both would have been on top running things now.

What is Papasan doing these days?

After he retired from the Yonkers Police Department he relocated to the Atlanta, Ga. area. He has taken his care for the youth and community with him. He currently has a dojo at the Recreation Center in Lithonia, Ga. the Brownsmill Recreation Center. Papasan finds it amusing that he grew up in Brownsville and he is raising kids in Brownsmill where he serves as the Director. Papasan can't get away from his hip-hop connection. Besides having a son that rapped, produced, and has dealt with DMX in the past. His most famous guest that came to the recreation center was T.I. T.I. came to the building when he had to do his community service for his gun charge. Papasan said that he spoke to the kids and he was pleased about what T.I. said that day. From Brownsville to Yonkers to Brownsmill, Georgia he is still showing a commitment to save lives.

Soke Papasan Canty 10th Degree Red Belt, Architect of the Kuroshi-Do System & Hall of Fame Martial Artist.

527/MULFORD GARDENS

Growing up in Mulford Gardens (MG) was cool. I loved it. I had wonderful experiences and memories. I learned about life, love, and the streets. I grew up most of my life in the projects thinking that this dude Keith was a "Godfather."

Why do I say that?

At the time he was doing some heavy hustling, it seems like he had the most respect, and he was holding the entire project down. He and his family were hustling at a young age and everyone was working for him. Then, I started watching how it was going down for real. I learned that life is a hustle, which is why I started hustling music. I saw the way the Yonkers hip-hop scene was going down, that's when I started doing parties with Truth & Divine, and the Tribal Brothers. I met them through my music hustle. I was doing all types of parties. One day divine asked who's the young kid doing all of these parties in town? Truth told him it was a young dude by the name of DJ Superior.

I lived at MG a long time. I started off at building 34 in the basement with my moms, and I remember the "Ghetto Rev" Raw Rome lived on the second floor, DJ Beat Master Gene was living in building 35, and DJ Kasun was living in building 33...look at all of that hip-hop in one place. I was blessed early being surrounded by major players in the game, which is why I had to fall in line.

Mulford was hard, but it also had a lot of love. Although there was an unspoken acceptance policy A.K.A. ghetto pass, outsiders were welcome to come. If you were accepted you were considered family, and you would feel like family. Don't forget DMX was from School Street but when he came to Mulford he got a lot of love. That is why he did most of those videos there, and he did a few on School Street. Mulford Gardens/527 was on another level, but there are people who would beg to differ. It's all good!

If we weren't the most feared we were the most respected. I remember on Halloween we used to have the battle of the projects, and we would have egg fights. We always won! We would sabotage the enemy. They would be peeking through the hood and wouldn't see anyone, when they finally were all the way in we would ambush them from the roof.

The same with the cops when they were chasing someone we would go to the roof, then go to another building and hide out in another apartment. If you grew up there as a kid there would be no way a cop can catch you unless they caught you slipping. They had to destroy that project because they couldn't manage it anymore. Musically that project nurtured many artists.

I remember watching Beat Master Gene do block parties and bring the hood together. People would come from all over Yonkers to chill out and there was no violence. I was taking a lot of notes while learning my craft. Back then Grant Park stayed packed.

Around that time I got into politics because when election time came around whoever was running for office started coming through the hood and showed a little respect. They would push their agenda, solicit votes for support, and make claims such as if we would put them in office they would do this or they would do that. From that time until now I haven't seen any real changes. Some may disagree but I challenge those to bring their facts on the differences. In my personal opinion President Obama has done more in his first 100 days of office than any other politician has done in my district or in Yonkers in the last five years. Many have come to Superior looking for support to get into office, and I have helped many of them. Unfortunately, overall they have done nothing.

I met people in the social/political circles when I was younger living in the projects while doing block parties. I would listen to everyone claim that they were doing something for the kids. When you hear people talking about the children, community, and youth most of the time it's a game. That's the easy way to get money. I have seen it with my own eyes just check out those running in your neighborhood you will find out most of them are running a game. It's an easy way to put money in people's pockets. I never associated with some of the locals for that very reason.

When I did an event I paid for everything I never asked anyone for anything. Plus, I provided everything free of cost. I recall doing the Wu-Tang party and I made about $12,000 I kept that money for so long I just kept on flipping it, and flipping it. Truth is my witness because I used to keep it under my mattress, and I would say to Jinx "You see this money this ain't from drugs this is from doing parties and busting my ass working." I let him know that he can do the same. It's crazy because growing up and even today everyone thought that we have to follow Scarface, Ghotti, and all the rest of these gangsters to make money and that's one of the biggest deceptions. Some of our rappers are pushing drugs to the kids, as well as having rappers wanting others to be drug dealers. You can't blame that one on the white man.

This is how I walked the dog at 527/Mulford Gardens: DMX used to stay at my house many nights, at that time X was getting high and robbing nigga's all throughout Yonkers he and his dog Boomer. He would be getting high at various places in the hood and I would go wherever he was and bring him home. It was like the movie "New Jack City" where I would go and get him from the spot. There would be base heads everywhere, and trust me it was not easy getting him out depending on where he was on any particular occasion. Sometimes getting him out was more difficult than other times, but because I loved him it was one of the things that I did for him; and I hated seeing him like that.

There were situations that would come up from his criminal activities that I had to deal with such as returning stolen property, or paying back money that X robbed from victims. Did he think that people was just going to allow him to rob them continuously and not get their belongings back? He was in the streets, in every hood in South West Yonkers just robbing people. Common sense would tell anyone that behavior would become dangerous quickly. There were people who said to me that by paying back Xs' debts I was encouraging his bad behavior and he would probably just continue. That was easy for some to say and that sounds like a line from a text book. There were many times when he knocked on my door in the morning and I didn't know what I was going to open the door to. At times he would show up with a ripped up shirt or I would see some blood on him. If you listen to his first album he will tell you how he was living.

I have seen the evidence of some of his songs that were already played out. Sometimes he used a knife, bat, or gun, but his preferred method was his dog Boomer. These were some of the chain of events that X was going through as he was developing his hip-hop craft prior to hitting the world with his music. Yonkers knew about him! While he was getting high he would be writing rhymes. He would come into the house writing while I was asleep, when I woke up he would record what he wrote, and then sell them that day. Mainly every day we would record...and that's how I would "Walk the Dog."

He took his styles and word play and developed his rhythm off old school break beats. It was nothing for him to drop those two platinum albums in a year. I still have several on stash. I did what I did for him because I knew he could possibly be someone big. He was so talented, but he had to get the monkey off his back.

I did what I did for him because he shared with me what happened to him years prior. He told me that it started when someone laced his weed that he used to get high with. One day he had his regular weed and he had gotten sick. That was unusual that his regular weed got him sick so he asked the dude who he was getting high with what did he put in it. The dude said crack! X told me that he tried to stop but he couldn't. The crack was the driving force. I know he was lacing his weed because if he was doing straight up crack he would have been dead by now.

I had a family member that was on drugs and she tried to rob me for my records. One day I came home and crates of my records are in the hallway stacked up, I was about to be cleaned out with all of my classics. It was a good thing I went straight home because I would have been a victim. One secret, if you don't already know is that when a crack head gets your belongings you have **slim to no chance** on getting it back. That's just how the game goes. I say all that to say X lived with me and never robbed me once, but my own family tried to do me in. X had love in the streets he could go anywhere and smoke. People would just give shit to him others were just paying him off because they didn't want to get a visit that night. That is another reason I knew he was talented because he would battle someone and literally be all fucked up and still rip 'em apart. That's why I kept "Walking the Dog" because it was just a matter of time.

Every dog has his day. We continued making those tapes and building our music stash then we will sell them, which is one of the ways X was able to support his habit. We would make music, press about 20 tapes and he was gone.

One day I called myself putting him on punishment by not producing any tapes for him, but it didn't work he would just go to another DJ. X went to Kool Jay and asked him to play some music for him, and Jay not knowing fell for his game. He couldn't read between the lines because X had such a powerful rep and his tapes were selling like crack. Then in no time the situation with X & Jay fell apart for whatever reason. It got so bad I had to give X some music and keep a stash for him because he didn't have any more. X started going around Yonkers selling blank tapes. He was telling who ever bought the tape that there was 60 minutes worth of music on there and it would be only one song. Some tapes would just be blank. Many people were angry with me because they knew I put the tapes together so they thought I was in on it.

Another shenanigan that took place is the amount of taxis that I would have to pay for him. He would just get in a taxi when he reached his destination he would just hop out. It took me a while to catch on to that one until one day when I heard someone cursing in Spanish. I went to see what was going on when I saw Papi standing in front of his taxi cursing and talking on the radio. Then a couple of minutes later X comes knocking on my door. One day X saw me paying his cab fare for him. He yelled at me and said "What the fuck you do that for; you're just wasting your money." He must not have realized or didn't give a damn that people knew he was coming to my house, which is why I had to keep the heat away from the crib.

JINX, SUPERIOR, & FRIEND

Many of the people in the area only saw one side of X. There was the daytime (sun) X and the night time (moon) X; I saw both sides that is why I stuck with him. I saw a lot of things and people would tell me things about him, but he never did those things to me that is why I couldn't judge him by the gossip and rumor mill. I don't judge people by what I hear about them such as people saying that dude is grimy, or that chick is a hoe. If you follow that rhetoric you can miss many opportunities rather than if you were to approach it in another way.

I learned from X that the people that talk about you the most will be shouting your name the loudest when you become successful. That was one of his motivations for success. That same principle is what I passed along to Jinx because he really looked up to X and wanted to follow in his footsteps. X didn't like Jinx in the beginning. He didn't like his flow, lyrics, he didn't like anything. Jinx was with a group called "The Midnight Thugs." It was all the same to X because he wasn't feeling them. He used to say to me "Those are your nigga's and I'm not fucking with them." I had to remind X of the fact that I didn't want to fuck with him in the beginning but look at us now. Remember Kasun was still locked down, and when I met him I only knew him for a year before he went to prison. However, I had enough sense to just follow the blueprint that Kasun laid, which was our recipe for success.

Shortly after we formed "Gangsters of the Ghetto" (G.O.G) I dealt with JLA who was talented, but he wanted to rap, DJ, and beat box that was the problem. He wanted to do every damn thing. He was a flashy dresser and a ladies' man. The only thing that made me upset is that he always wanted to be seen.

GANGSTER OF THE GHETTO

(G.O.G.)

BM was another rapper that was with us. At the time he and X had problems because he was BM and X was DM. Of course X was not feeling that and Little Assassin (Steve Streets) just went with the flow. We practiced hard and continued to develop our craft. I eventually ran into this dude named Tiny who brought WA to meet X. From day one he was feeling X. He put X in battles and wanted him. He knew I had the music, which is why he had to deal with me too. The situation was good it was all love.

Of course something crept in that made the situation greasy because we had a deal with Columbia Records and Columbia really wanted DMX. X put out a single with them called "Born Loser." We also had a street song circulating on the streets called "The Mary song," which was dissing Mary J. Blige. The reason why we did that was to show the streets that if we thought someone was dissing or not showing respect to Yonkers we were blasting them. X and I were on a rampage at that time. Those were just some of the things we were up to.

MARY J. BLIGE & SUPERIOR

As time passed I found out that Columbia also wanted to sign me to a deal. The unfortunate thing is I wasn't informed about this until eight years later. We were in the Ruff Ryders office talking and WA said "They wanted to sign you too," and I said well why didn't anyone tell me about it? No one had an answer for me. That pissed me off, but I shook it off and said maybe it wasn't for me to be an artist. I continued working behind the scenes, and I kept "Walking the Dog." We were getting closer to getting out there we had a foot in the door so we went harder. As X started getting closer or as the door was opening up more and more X started flipping on me, and we started to clash. He would come by asking me for songs and I would ask him what the plan was. I was sitting on over 300 songs that we had recorded at the crib. However, I knew something wasn't right because X was acting differently. It wasn't us anymore he kept on talking about himself, which is why I asked him, "Well what am I going to be doing?" "What role am I going to be playing?" X is always straight up, and now I am not getting any direct answers from him.

He was dissing me talking a lot of shit and in a matter of days or couple of weeks he gets locked up again. Now, I'm his main man again, his best boy, "Dogs for Life." This time when he was gone I had to take care of that crazy dog **Boomer**. X starts writing me letters from jail with instructions of all of the things that he wanted me to do with the music. He kept emphasizing that I take care of business; but I distinctly remember a couple of days earlier he was cussing me out. He was stating those are my tapes, my music, my this, and my that. He was on a real ego trip. Now, look what he wrote to me in the letter.

LETTER FROM DMX TO MIKE SUPERIOR

(1)

Yo Superior,

What's up nigga? Besides all the bullshit, how have you been? Yo I knew I could count on you to take care of things for me. I don't have to worry about Bonnie because you gave me your word and I know that she's alright.

Yo don't even stress the business. Do what you can, and whatever you can't we'll take care of together when I come home. You're a good brother and you will be rewarded ten-fold. Also don't even worry about what niggas say about me, because they never say it to me. My system is clean and it's going to stay that way. Remind me to tell you why I slipped last time. Everyday I realize while watching videos, that I really could be right up there with them. I have a lot of new material and I'm going to do something with it before it gets old. I'm tired of writing shit and having it go to waste. I feel like I'm being wasted along with my talent. It's very frustrating. I know that I have something that people want

LETTER FROM "X" FROM JAIL

This time when he was gone I had to take care of Boomer the dog. Boomer was trained like a K9 dog that the police have except he was for the streets. There was a certain time at night when Boomer would become wild in the house, and I would have to take him outside otherwise he would tear the house apart. Then, I remembered that he was a hood K9 and he patrolled in the moonlight or midnight. When I took him out for a walk he would guide me different places. I noticed that every time he saw the police he would stop, look around and try to hide; or when we would pass certain people he would bark and growl. It was as though he knew who to stick up, and I can tell that he enjoyed the sport with X. When Boomer saw sirens he would react just like a person getting chased by the police. The first time I experienced it he almost broke my arm trying to make a move. People used to see me with Boomer and start taking off their jewelry and going inside their pockets. I was like this dog is going to get me killed! I had an idea of how X was getting his money, but the time I spent with Boomer really filled in a lot of the blanks.

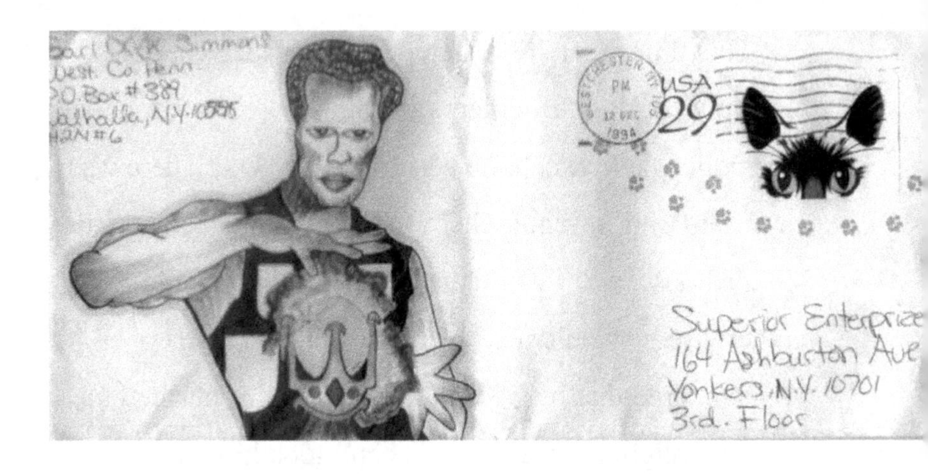

LETTER FROM DMX TO SUPERIOR

X needed material for his album when he is released from jail; and now, he's on some other stuff. He begins to throw his muscle around trying to get people to hurt me and rob me for the music. Dudes in Yonkers were like we know the deal how are we going to step to you and you were holding him down? I wouldn't have even heard about the dude if it wasn't for your mixed tapes. They were saying that kid Superior never did anything to us, right is right and wrong is wrong. That is what he got back from the streets but in *paragraph 2 of the 1st letter he sent me from jail* 'he said he will bless me tenfold'. I never ran I was still at Mulford and School 12. I used to send messages on my mixed tapes telling them that they knew where I lived and where I worked and what time I got off. It's all recorded and accessible.

After all of that I started doing parties really hard doing my own thing. I set a party up for him and Wu-Tang and I put X on the card to perform, but what I didn't appreciate was him disrespecting Wu-Tang. He was like "Fuck those nigga's I'm DMX, I run this town." I know one thing that whatever he said pissed off RZA and they were about to fuck X up! Bottom line is I created and promoted parties and busted my ass to get his name out there. That was before Ruff Ryders came to Yonkers. All my marketing, promotion, and business structure came from an old white woman named Julie Wilson that had my back!!

I knew I was rising to another level when I started having problems with my own people in the projects. At the time there was a group in town called the Tribal Brothers. X was still doing his thing, but I was playing him from a distance. I really wasn't worried because what I created in X, I could create in something or someone else. I was working more with Jinx, and the Tribal Brothers.

The experience with the Tribal Brothers was good, but as life goes I had a problem with one of the brothers in the group. He used to talk all of the time about this brother man stuff. In the back of my mind I never felt as though he was there with us. Keep in mind every crew goes through something. We used to meet at the house, but all of the meetings were about money. Paying dues becoming a strong unit all of those things are cool, but it was a bit fishy to me because I couldn't see where the money was going. When I asked I couldn't get any answers and was labeled a trouble maker. After a while they were stepping off one by one. The members that stepped off had problems with the same person. However, I stuck it out to show that clown that he didn't move me like that. I wanted to show him that he couldn't pimp me with his scriptures, which is why I dealt with him head to head to the end. That's how I was at a young age. There was one dude that was his flunky and he wanted me to follow in those footsteps. Guess what? I wasn't having it. After he learned that his scriptures couldn't control me he called me a rebel. As I got older I realized he was a "scripture pimp". I learned that sometimes you have to walk your own path because people look to prey on the weak. I still never found out where the money went.

Eventually, I purchased my own system and that dude didn't want to be around me. He preached power, unity, and coming up, however when I got my own system he started flipping. You have some leaders that produce leaders and you have some leaders who produce and want followers. To this day we don't see eye to eye, but as the saying goes...it is what it is!

In that apartment at 527 Mulford Gardens we also dreamed of Def Jam and we entertained the idea of starring in movies.

What my mother did to me prepared me I just didn't know it. My mother hustled up enough money to put clothes on our back so that we can look descent, and we were well taken care of by a single mother. As time went on my mother wanted to have fun, this is what made me put the shield around myself in my life, and I put the metal all around my skin. If it wasn't for my mom I wouldn't have survived everything that I have been through in Yonkers and especially what I have been through with X.

One day my mother gave me two month's rent and moved down South and left me and told me that I have to take care of myself. I didn't have anything at the time, I was going through hard times and had X and Jinx living in the house. Those were the times that we were talking about becoming really big and getting on Def Jam we had it all figured out even the acting part. That's all we talked about I was doing artist development before I actually realized what it was. I was upset with Ruff Ryders because they knew what I did for X and they should have done something for me in their company. I used to run with Swiss back then we spent some time together and as time went along we separated. Maybe he thought I wanted something from him but we were boys once upon a time.

I'm always asked how come I know so many millionaires and none of them ever reach out to me? What did I do to them?

My answer is always I didn't do anything to them. It's hard looking at all of these guys on TV, because after a while you begin to think that maybe it was something I did or didn't do. I begin to question myself. If you're weak you can become depressed and develop an inferiority complex that can stunt your growth. I took a bad situation and used it to motivate me, which is why I named my company "Most Hated." My rationale was in order for those people to do what they did to me over and over again I must be the "Most Hated."

I was a team player all the way I always gave 110%. I didn't demonstrate practices of disloyalty so what was the problem. I kept on looking in the mirror and I asked myself why do I love those that don't love me? Why am I helping those that don't help me? So, I put my experience and talent into building myself up, and now when I'm looked at by those who did me wrong they ask me what's my problem? I tell them that I'm the product you created. I'm something you raised, and do not be mad at your creation. I'm not blaming everyone only the people who had the power to change situations and make things happen. I worked with them and they did me wrong. But as the saying goes...that was then and this is now.

THEY DID ME WRONG

I realized that my mom did me wrong as well. I realize that it's hard for a woman to raise a boy into a man, but she still did me wrong. What makes it so bad is that she did me wrong several times. One time it was because of a man, another time was because she didn't believe me, lastly, she sent me away to a group home. I have a lot of stories, but I will share this one in particular.

One day I found out that the man she was dating at the time was fondling one of my nieces. That situation separated us because she was in denial. My own mother didn't want to listen to me or even look at the evidence; and to make matters worse she took his side and turned on me.

School 12 has also done me wrong because of the history that I have with them, and all the good things that I did. In my opinion I should be one of the people running the joint, instead they have taken advantage of the love and care that I have for the community and the young people. They raped my resources and ideas along the way and only paid me $25,000 per year. I saved many lives and helped make effective change in more youth than the top 5 counselor's in Yonkers put together. I wonder if hard work and dedication count for anything.

I sat in on many executive board meetings, in many social circles, and someone always has something to say about team work. However, from experience I see that it is rarely recognized or appreciated. It's all lip service.

My pops also did me wrong, which is why I hate when someone calls me by my legal (government) name!

There are people who would ask me why I hate having my father's name and it is simply because he named me Mike, and we were his family my mother, sister, and me. Then, he simultaneously started another family and named his other son Mike. What type of shit is that? You have to remember I experienced all of this as a young child. This is the reason I'm called Superior. When I tell people that I have a brother named Mike they become confused, and the really inquisitive ones start putting the pieces together. So, I just stopped using the name.

All of you grimy slime balls that dealt with me from the bottom of the deck I have learned to use those tools as motivation toward my success.

Thank you!!

PUT THEM ON BLAST

This chapter is self-explanatory I'm going to start off with Kasun. I met Kasun when I was young and doing parties trying to come up and aspiring to do something different with my life. He taught me a valuable business lesson that I will never forget and I would like to thank him.

Years ago I was involved in the first DMX/Bill Blass battle at School 12 and the only reason why we got the place is because I worked there and I was connected. Bottom line the place was packed the crowd spilled into the streets of Ashburton. When it was all said and done he gave me about $40, that instance right there made me see how money changes things. It made me realize how I had to develop my hustle and business savvy. The jewel that I took away from that experience is that you can make the recipe for the pie, buy the ingredients, and even bake it; but that doesn't mean that you're going to necessarily get to eat it.

Shortly after that he caught a case and went up North. While he was away I picked up the torch and ran with DMX and it was on from there. Kasun taught me not to depend on anyone and handle business on my own terms. He was business savvy and very impressionable to a young man. If I didn't cross paths with Kasun at that time and hooked up to do those battle parties, I wouldn't have had the opportunity to have developed my relationship with X.

As far as Truth is concerned he's a big brother that I never had he helped me out a lot. I wish he would have stepped up and spoke up for me when I was in those circles being played by those devils. He taught me a few things, but intentionally left a few things out, which I didn't find out until I was older. With his history in the game if he would have done things a little different he would be in a better situation right now.

As for DJ Lil Jay he also helped me out when I was getting my ass kicked at Brown Eyes club one night. I was trying to protect DJ Kool T and I winded up getting jumped by about 5-7 guys. When you're on the ground getting kicked and stomped you really don't know how many people are kicking you. After a while all of the boots start looking and feeling the same. What Lil J did was he used his body to shield me from the attackers. He helped save my life, out of hundreds of people that were there that night only Truth and Jay helped me. What made the situation so bad is those kids were from Mt. Vernon.

A lot of those dudes didn't get along, but in public it's all smiling faces because the regime I was rolling with, which was Tribal Brothers had beef with Beat Master Gene. The head of the team that I was rolling with was orchestrating everything; he was using everyone like we were his puppets. This is the reason I was angry with Truth because he could have squashed all of it.

The beef that I had with Disco Rick could have been prevented and we possibly wouldn't have had the brawl at the cook out on Jones Place. I don't know his exact role, but he knew those kids that beat me down at Brown Eyes. He used to role with BMG, but the circle of dudes that I was with kept on spitting venom in my ear about him, Tribal Brothers was cool but some of the practices were questionable.

DJ Good Times was always cool he was a good guy that stayed to himself and did his own thing an old school pioneer that made things happen, I learned a lot from him.

I can't forget Irv Gotti who hit me with no Vaseline, why do I say that? Because back in the day X and I made a song at my house called "Niggas can't touch me kid," and it was really hot in the streets. At that time the newly formed Ruff Ryders needed a hot song for X so we went into the studio and re-did the song. We had it pressed up and everything, and when it was all said and done Irv Gotti put his name on the record as the Executive Producer and he didn't do **SHIT**!

J. B.is questionable and I see him as a slimy so called leader. He started off as a good man, and I think he used to have good intentions, but on the other side he's suspect. You see there are street rules and community rules and the truth is that what they are calling gang violence in Yonkers Mr. B feels and claims that he knows how to stop and handle it. However, one day when I met with him I told him that the more he promotes gang violence the more people are going to want to do it, and the more it's going to spread. If I'm a child watching the news and I am constantly hearing about meetings on gang violence, the coverage alone are leaving impressions in my head. I think it's a sophisticated way of promoting oneself to push his personal political agenda. In the long run I don't think that would be the remedy for the community.

If I was a young man trying to get a reputation I would form my own gang and do things in the hood to get noticed and have people talk about me. The streets are watching and they are really smart. Mr. B is sending out the wrong message. The message he should be sending out is that we are not going to tolerate gangs and that's it! Trust me if there was no funding there would be no talking. In my opinion Mr. B is just a political pimp.

The female political leader for the community overall is a good woman. When I was a young man I had to give her a wakeup conversation about different things going on in the community that she needed to become aware of. People were dying all around her and she needed help. I knew that she couldn't fix all of the problems in the neighborhood but as a politician she can represent the district that voted her in. It's deeper than calling her office reaching the secretary and the secretary is claiming that she's booked. Why would she always be booked? When the camera is on its all smiles, but all situations do not require a smile. How can you be happy all of the time?

I grew up looking up to certain black leaders in the community that held political positions of power, and I was under the illusion that everyone who shared my pigmentation had our best intentions at hand. As I got older and a little wiser I realized that was just a myth, a cruel hoax. I wish America was everything I thought it was, and also what the media propaganda and educational institutions say that it is. I feel as though if children could run this country it would be a better place.

I wanted to be like a lot of those people that I looked up to, but as I lived life and interacted with some of my childhood role models I discovered that some of them are just wolves in sheep's clothing...that's scary, really scary!

They are our representatives and they are the ones in power. It's amazing because everyone wants you to be positive, put your best foot forward, and lead by example that is why my resume is geared towards up-liftment for the community. I have sent several invitations to a few influential people in town and I get no response, and no show; however, if something terrible happens in the town everyone is all over it I'm confused.

I had a bunch of children help one of the officials get into office; we went all out to make sure that this person got into that position. The position is really powerful and since she was elected I haven't heard from her since. I sat on the board with this person at School 12, and you would think that she would at least drop a line once in a while. It's sad but it goes to show that people from other races helped me out and have given me more chances than my own people.

I would like to thank the late Mayor Zaleski for giving me a job. I was on his staff for two years, which was a great experience being young and working for the mayor. How many people get to experience that?

Julie Wilson was also a white woman who gave me an opportunity to grow. During our interaction we helped each other grow. Through our interaction I was able to bring The Wu Tang Clan and other groups to town. She also taught me how to develop my music and hustle, and I'm forever grateful to her. These days I don't really help people become elected because I'm tired of getting used by these blood suckers. I have worked with and have been taught by the best; therefore, I'm not buying what they are selling.

Let's not forget the dude that was but naked and tied up to a chair in the studio. You keep running your mouth I'm going to leak the video and finish your career.

Lastly, I would like to apologize to Beat Master Gene for the wrong that I have done to him, because I was ignorant and young and was lead to believe that he and other popular DJ's in Westchester were my enemy. I have learned that just because someone has a different social circle and may have different ways than yourself you shouldn't alienate them. Through this experience I have learned to open my mind and heart.

RELATIONSHIP & LOVE

I'm good at a lot of things, but I am no good at the relationships. It may sound sad, but I just don't connect well. How can I do something that wasn't done for me? Basically, I don't get too close to women if something happens, then it happens. I was so bad that in the past I used to have a one page contract drawn up that was short and to the point. I told the women that it was a temporary mess around thing, so that they couldn't say that I was a dog or that I was using them. I laid it all out in the beginning and I would get their signature on the document. I had a bunch of rules that I created that had been working over the years.

Rule #1: No acting out in the street.
Rule#2: We're not really a couple, etc.

Having a contract most women responded very well they seemed to all want that. Some of the women wanted the contract because they had situations involving a boyfriend that they didn't want to give up. Other women just wanted to have sex; whatever the situation, you can draw up your own agreement to suit the situation. There are women who will do things with their side-man that they wouldn't do with their main-man. I have met women who have planned very well, they have a spare or a backup plan, which is where I come in, and am very comfortable with that. I am the fall back man!

I have only had three girlfriends in my life. One girlfriend had a lot of money, but she wanted to buy me and take control over my life. One example of her controlling ways is back in the days when I would have to hit the streets and DJ she would ask me how much I was getting paid, and if I told her $300 she would offer me $500. After a while the roles seemed to be changing as though she was the man and I was the woman. She wanted to do everything because she had so much money.

I hear a lot of men say that they want a situation like that, but if they ever came across something like that they would quickly reevaluate the situation in a couple of days. She paid my rent for six months up front. She taught me how to save money, the only problem I had is that I wouldn't commit. As we were still dating she started dating this other dude, and I ran up on him at the barbershop on Ashburton and confronted him. When I tried to get at him, and grab him he hid behind her. The cops were called because it was alleged that I had a gun, but the Truth was there that day and he knew how it went down. I did a month for that in Valhalla. I was stressed and didn't want to be there, I thought my crib was being robbed because she had a key to my crib. Plus, there were some grimy janitors up in the hood some of the robberies that were taking place in the hood were definitely inside jobs. Yes, believe it the maintenance men were or are dirty!

They would case your place when they're fixing the toilet or general maintenance duties, and when you're gone they would go in with their key. I have some of those incidents on tape. I caught a janitor going into my refrigerator and helping himself to some cool aid. I had hidden cameras in my house that's why no one involved can deny how they really got down. I had my bedroom, kitchen and living room under surveillance where I had a chance to see how people really get down when you're not around.

You may have a woman that says she loves you, says she's behind you, and says she will do anything to support you; however, as soon as you leave the house she's on the phone talking about you to her friends. She is saying things to her girlfriends like I'm going to milk this nigga and take his money, or I'm about to go and meet this other guy. It sounds crazy, but it's real, and that's where the Most Hated comes in because of the things that I have done. The worst thing you can do to me is to lie to me because I never forget, and somewhere down the line I'm going to get you back.

I had a girlfriend that started lying, and cheating on me. Here is a situation that I will never forget…the day I actually caught my girlfriend in the park having sex with another man. I caught them in the grass doggie style. I knew she was there because of a conversation that she had with her girlfriend, and her girlfriend called me and told me what was going down. You see what I mean when I say everyone is always plotting. I took that information and ran with it! She had just bought our wedding rings, and we were about to take our relationship to the next level when I caught her. She had the nerve to ask me how I knew she was there. Why was I in the park? How long have I been up there? I wanted to smack her up, but I'm not into that. I did rip off her top when I snatched her up, then I took her ring off as I did mine and threw them both in the grass. It was over! It was too much for me to handle and this time it was a different man, not the same one I got into it with at the barbershop.

There are people who may ask, don't you think about all of the time you spend running around with "X" that you should have been handling your business with your woman? Ultimately if you don't another dude will! The answer to that would be no, that wasn't the reason she was trying to strong arm me into marriage. I had someone watching her, and their job was to inform me about who, what, where, and when, he had no other job. I wanted to know exactly what I was working with, and at that point in my life I didn't have trust in anyone. I thought everyone was trying to get close to me to get access to the hidden DMX Masters, I was paranoid. And, not even my sister can get too close because of the rumors of her dealing with someone in the Ruff Ryder's camp. I wouldn't think my sister would set me up, but she could have been used as a pawn. There was a situation that occurred that has caused us not to get along until this very day.

One day my sister came to my house with several guys from Ruff Ryders camp. No one knew that I had cameras posted on my window and all around the building. I had the cameras set up at School 12, and at my apartment. In Mulford I had about four cameras from different angles, not because I was scared, it was because I had different people coming by some I knew others I didn't. I was told by J.B. that he once told those dudes with my sister that Superior will know that y'all came by. The guys that were with my sister left abruptly and got back into their car once they heard that I had cameras. They got into their cars and drove away, which made my sister a little suspect. I didn't know what was what, because at times people down with the Ruff Ryders made me feel as though they were going to just come and take my shit if/or when the chance presented itself; their bosses wouldn't treat me like that. Sometimes you have people trying to show off for the boss trying to come up and make a name for themself, it becomes confusing sometimes.

The last woman that I cared about and lost a lot of respect for, now we are close. The problem with her is that she wanted me to change too much. She wanted me to stop doing music, but when she met me I was knee deep into the game. She told me to stop dealing with one of the artists. She didn't like when she saw things that were talked about in the media and my contributions were not mentioned. She knew I busted my ass and gave 110%. We went to baby showers and brought gifts to people and their children when no one else was thinking to do the same. It used to tear her apart and she couldn't take it anymore me not being honored, she would push for me to work at a club to be a DJ downtown Manhattan for someone else. She never overstood the Most Hated concept of self-employment and empowerment of those around me, I wouldn't settle for less.

There was a time when her girlfriends got into her head with, if he doesn't get you a ring or doesn't even think about getting you a ring by this time that must mean…he really doesn't love you. They were all in her head! About a month before we broke up I told her sister that I was looking for a ring. Her sister was fair and balanced and that's what I loved about her. I was trying to mend the relationship, which is why I bought her a truck and put down on a ring to try and make things better; but she claimed that I wasn't affectionate or caring. I was just trying to complete my task. I don't get it most people want a go getter, but most don't really understand what really comes with the territory. Reality shows have their brains twisted.

Everyone seems to concentrate on the end result and what happens in between doesn't matter; that's what happens when you're on a mission, and you're only focused on the end result. We had been through a few things together, and I thought she was my road-dog through thick and thin.

There was a time when we would leave our phones out; then she started sleeping with the phone under her pillow. I started wondering what was going on, which is why I felt as though I had to get to her phone. It took a minute, but when I finally got my hands on it I realized there was one number that kept showing up. Then, I looked at the text messages and said to myself… man she's messing with that wing? It was someone that I knew that I can break up really bad, but I wouldn't touch him because he's weak and it would hurt my name more than it would help. The fact remained that he was spitting game to my girl. He was texting things like "I can't wait to touch that booty," "I'm going to spank you today." I knew it was going to go down between him & me.

Our relationship changed her conversation was switching up. She would say things like you need to do this or I will do that. She started taking trips, and when her girlfriends asked her where is Superior she told them he was busy or she would plant other negative seeds in their head about me. A lot of her friends were telling her she needed to cut things off with me. Meanwhile they didn't have the real story.

I didn't let her know about the truck until she packed up and left the crib and was in her new spot. She also wasn't aware that I had two places to live just in case something comes up. However, on this occasion I let her stay in one of the other apartments because I couldn't let her be homeless. I didn't do her dirty but I could have. All of the different women in my life taught me something. One of the women was really street; one smoked a lot of cigarettes and was gangster which was too much for me.

I just want people to remember that some of the people you see on TV have a supporting staff, you don't hear about them. If you're a man like me you have to grind, and no I can't be in the house by 6:00pm. Her new man must be a sucker to go for that. But, I gave thought to where I got her from; she was previously with my man D-Bow who treated her like shit. He said he was just hitting it, I think he even gave her a sexually transmitted disease. Therefore, mentally I think she came to me with issues and I inherited all of the bullshit. I'm just looking for someone who can stand on their own two feet; I don't want to be anyone's crutch. How can they help me when I'm carrying them?

Watching my mother growing up I remember hearing the story about my mother catching my father in the house with another woman in her bedroom having sex. My mother told me that she went into the kitchen, boiled some hot water, and threw it on my father. She said that she didn't do anything to the other woman, but told her to get the hell out of the house, as my father was still under the cover trying to protect himself from the hot water screaming and yelling. I don't want my children growing up in a situation like that.

I used to tell those women that if we have a child I'm going to be there for them if not then we can't do it. With black families there are just so many dynamics that cause division in the family. America promotes cheating and going to the strip clubs they make reality shows about that. Growing up I needed the father figure. My mother did the best that she could until she got tired of me and left. I had to fend for myself in this mean world.

Now, let me speak about my child's mother (A.K.A. baby's mom). They all say that they want a man, who cares, shows concern, emotion, hardworking, and

Me And My Daughter

SUPERIOR & DAUGHTER

everything else, but in some cases that's still not enough! The relationship between man and woman on the planet now in my eyes has been tarnished and is in need of serious repair. It's all messed up all the way around, you have so many women nowadays that are playing out the roles of a man; or there are the women who listen to their girlfriends and can't think for themselves. I wonder how a woman who doesn't have a man can tell a woman with a man how to handle her affairs?

Honestly, I think more women need to stand by their men more often, and be supportive. I waited a long time to have a child because I didn't want to bring a child into this world and have it become another me. I took my time because I wanted to breed another type of person in the next generation. I had a dream like Martin, but she didn't hang in there with me. We had some hard times in our relationship and I had to make ends meet. I had to make a way to provide for our family, and I did that but that still wasn't enough.

She kept throwing in my face the fact that DMX is signed now and when are you going to get your share?

After a while that became a regular argument. She was throwing that up in my face every chance that she had, eventually she split. As I look back I now realize that you really don't know what people's intentions are.

BECOMING A MAN

Going from a teenager to becoming a man was extremely hard for me. I didn't have any elders or brothers around to walk and guide me through the experience. I remember looking around and seeing my friends with men around helping them. At that time I had no one. People always say that there is always someone I could have gone to. That's not always the case. Sometimes your street family treats you better than your actual blood family. There were many things that I wanted for myself and couldn't have. That's why I promised when I had children I was going to show them a different way.

Becoming a man you learn that sometimes you have to make sacrifices. I knew I was becoming a man by the way that I handled all of the disrespect given to me when X was signed to Def Jam. Before DMX was signed to Def Jam people say he wasn't shit, and always made sure they threw up the word crack head. As soon as they heard he signed a contract, now the whole Yonkers loved DMX.

A man has discipline of his mind and actions. I learned that sometimes you just have to walk away, and not allow anger to take over your mind causing you to make the wrong decision (the red light). They say the more money the more problems, but let's not forget the more money involved the bigger demons that are involved. I witnessed that first hand. It seems as though people would do anything for fame and money. What's sad about it is they will come up with logical explanations to justify doing shady underhanded things. All under the guise of trying to make money, but they always say this is business nothing personal. I had to think about that so in the name of business I'm justified to do anything to get it. Even to my loved ones and the people who have been in my corner all of my life. That's an interesting business concept I wonder who came up with that. Just look at the word business it is spelled Bu-sin-ess and smack right there in the middle is the word sin!

I have seen people do real dirty, greazy things to each other for money. Many people front like they are religious, but their real religion is money. They should just be straight up with it. What's sad is people never think about the sayings or phrases that they model their life after, and that's what the industry looks for, people that do anything for money. They will reel them in, start to manipulate, and take control of their lives. So what X did to me I just brushed it off because regardless of what others think I know he knows the real deal.

At the time I wasn't concerned about myself I was just telling him to look out for Jinx. Finally, Jinx caught the attention of X by following in X's footsteps battling rappers in the Westchester area (refer to the DVD Straight out of Yonkers). When Jinx was finally signed to bloodline records we started to play it smart because X became flaky on us, and tried to turn us against each other. He would say one thing to one of us and something different to the other. He didn't know every night we were on the phone discussing what was really going on. That's when it got really sad because we started acting as though we were falling for his nonsense. He wanted that fake shit so we gave him that fake shit! These guys in town kill me. When you hear these lyrics about how real they are their people are this, their hood is that but it is not what it appears to be. These artists have the same tactics and practices as a seasoned politician just check it out! My situation is that I trained a multimillionaire and did a lot of things to protect him, some of, which I will not talk about in the book or at least not this one. All he had to do was to throw a dog a bone. I can name people on both hands that came in and capitalized off the DMX phenomenon.

Back at 57 Mulford Gardens before the fame we just talked about the movies, businesses, and even opening a club. After "Get at me Dog" he didn't want to do any of the above, or at least not with me. I even have that recorded! What's funny is that when he was hot he didn't care about the footage, he was like fuck the footage it's yours, and you rock with that. One day you're going to get paid off that shit. I was like alright. Then, the 180^0 came and he started going downhill, all of a sudden he comes to me with his gangster strong arm tactics trying to get the music. I was like you got my stuff now I have your stuff.

We had more than enough material to make Bloodline successful, we had a lot of talent just the wrong hands in the pot! I had a nice position with Def Jam it came with an office plus the bells and whistles. We did "The

Cradle to the Grave," "The Great Depression," after that they said that the budget money was all used up. The gangsters in the suits are more vicious than the gangsters in the streets. Think about it you are around sharks that are well seasoned in the business, and they gave a drug addict a multimillion dollar budget. What do you think is going to happen? It's true that his people were not in a position to monitor what was really going on, which is why they did him dirty. He had people robbing him blind when he started Bloodline records. I guess that came with a group of new devils.

Ruff Ryders business practices was a little too strong arm for him, but at the same time they put him out there, and took him out of the hood. You can always negotiate, but in the new circle it was filled with many ghouls and yes men. In no time he was way out there too far gone and I was there with him. Every time I said something or made a comment I was always hit with Superior has a problem with this, and Superior has a problem with that. I thought I was watching his back because he didn't see what was really going on.

We watched an $8 million dollar budget that was given to us to put the label together just disappear. Just because they give you a budget doesn't mean that they are going to use all of the money that they were going to give you for the project. It's all business! There are some artists who are a priority to the label, and you have some throw-aways.

Someone may ask what I mean by **a throw away**.

A throw away is an artist assigned to a record label that's never going to have a career of his own. He is just there to rep. the group and promote, and is used for tax write-offs. They are so caught up in the fame they don't even know that they are being used. An example of this is "Flip Mode Squad." Busta Rhymes came out and did his thing, but they had an artist on the label named Baby Sham and he was managed by my man named Jermani. We have a gold plaque on the wall because the album went gold. Jermani was trying his best to get Baby Sham a solo deal, and when Busta found out he fired Jermani. At the time Jermani thought that his job was to make things better for the artist, then he realized in the music game things are not what they appear to be. An example of this would be: In the United States we use cows for milk to drink, and also use cows for meat.

Some artists have to come to the conclusion that they are just part of the cattle (going to slaughter). They manipulate your desire for stardom and you keep waiting for your turn that never comes. At the same time you become more loyal, but you're just a tax write-off. Baby Sham never came out, but Ra Digga came out! Females on the label always get a chance to shine most of the time. With our situation at Bloodline we had seven artists and the chances of any of them getting a solo album were slim. I knew some of them were cattle. I just kept pushing Jinx and was told I was out of script.

We had many good artists in our camp besides Jinx; we also had Iceburg also known to the world as **Young Burg**. We never put him out on Bloodline, but when he left the camp he dropped two successful albums. Maybe Xs' intentions were good for Bloodline, but the powers that be didn't give a damn. That's why I give Roc-A-Fella and G-Unit credit. Regardless of how people feel about them their artist will always eat; and their artists always have release dates for their albums. Now, let me take it back home this is a touchy story, but I'm in search of the facts. I have to address the question, what really happened with J-Hood?

There are many experiences that have helped me become a man another example is with the Tribal Brothers. That was a gift and a curse. Some people want to lead you to water and show you the water, but as soon as you try to take a cup they say not yet, it's not cold enough. For reasons such as that I'm wired to help young men become men.

I've seen the effects of people with no supporting casts at the home. 80% of the artists around me don't have the presence of their father in their life. Every situation is different you just have to be a good listener. Some may have a father in their life, but he may be on drugs, or destroyed by other social ills that plague the city. Others may have fathers that are locked away in jail, every story is different! Some situations may have a mother and father, but they still don't have the necessary skills to keep the kids protected from the social ills.

I have been helping youths for over 20 years, and I have a successful track record. I helped people that were coming from the jail and prison, that were on parole and obligated to do community service. They did their service at my facility. It disgusts me when celebrities set up these foundations that look good for press, but are really ineffective in saving lives.

A general practice of mine is that I put youth together that don't know one another. In situations like that it creates friendships, bonds, knocks down barriers, and builds relationships, after they realize that they are all going through the same thing. I found to unlock the misery is to bring them together, because this world keeps us so divided. When I was a youth director or counselor my job didn't end at 5:00pm. The only time that happens is if you are only in it for a paycheck. You don't make a lot of money so you have to be in it with your heart. That is the trade off!

Some people care but they don't care that much. Some people only care when the camera is on, or when they want some press. I was really there for the kids 24 hours a day, and also dealing with X at the same time. It helped me become a man because I had to sacrifice. I lost a lot of women dealing with X. One chick thought I had to be smoking as well; she thought I was an undercover crack head. Another chick would be paranoid when X came to the house, she stayed far away from him, and kept the door closed and locked. She couldn't understand that I only wanted him to do well.

There are billions of people on Earth, but very few match his talents. Very few have had the opportunity to be in his midst, such as the privileged position that I was in. I see it as though I found a bad puppy that was limping and needed nursing. I bandaged him up and gave him some brotherly love. When he became well and signed a contract people came out of the wood work, and wanted to know if he was eating, was he alright, and all of that fake insincere bullshit. However, my job was 24 hours a day; I dealt with the daytime X and the night time X. None of them had the guts to come around when the moon came out. I was also 24 hours for Jinx, because at the time his older brother was going through situations. Jinx was going through it, but he had a strong mother. He just came to me because he knew I provided the music, and he was hungry. Plus, I was a big brother to him and X.

Jinx success in music was my success, because no one would have ever thought that he would get out of the projects and do anything especially being featured on any platinum albums. I felt good when he was featured on "Cradle to the Grave," because I made that happen through Bloodline. At least something good came out of that label for someone else in the camp. I put Jinx on the same formula that I had X on. Marlon from the Sporty Thievz was on the formula before he joined their camp.

Also, I had Phill Blunts in the camp at the time when he was supposed to sign to Mary's label, but nothing came out of that situation. I would take the underdog and make them champions. I would be with the guys that everyone would be dissing, and turn it around where those same people will buy music and pay to see you perform. X had people that he used to rob show up at his release party buying his cd, and anything else they could get their hands on.

What else helped me become a man is the Bully situation, because I developed him, created a buzz, and even pushed him overseas. Eventually, D-Block comes out of nowhere and starts offering him things. I'm thinking that he was going to stay loyal, because I busted my ass for him, but the stars in his eyes had him blind.

When people think they're going to get fame most will sell you out for less than nothing. Nowadays, I know how the scenario plays out. Some of the artists in my past we didn't have a contract together. The situation I had with Bully was like that because I saw something in him. I had a contract on Jinx because DMX was trying to take him from me. I find that funny because at the beginning he couldn't stand him. When I am on your side, I am on your side.

As of now I have three people living with me because of their unfortunate circumstances. I'm not saying I'm a magnet to attract people in messed up situations; but I give off a vibe that can be picked up, and when it's read the translator of the message realizes I just will not let people sit there and die. Like the hypocrites in the power structure! If someone offered me a job paying $80K working with the youth, or running a record label I would choose the youth because it's more rewarding to me.

I did have Bully under a management contract, and he still went to D-Block. I know he is not signed to them as an artist, but he must be signed to them as something else. According to my sources it was done that way, because they didn't know what I was going to do in the future. Now, behind the scenes Bully is a good man. In the beginning we had this plan I wanted him to be with D-Block but he wanted D-Block and Most Hated, because he didn't want to be in the same situation as J-Hood. I was his back up. After the money and the glory came, followed by the women, once that happened the loyalty was gone! The love turns to disrespect and they begin to try to turn others against you. Some may not like my personality, but you cannot deny my works with the youth, and music. I don't have a college degree, but I know many people with degrees that are unemployed, or really don't make a mark on this world.

Then you have a person like DMX that took street college and became a multimillionaire. I was the underdog and maybe that's why X and I connected. As he was robbing everyone left and right I was behind him trying to make things better. After a while it seemed as though some people began to accept being robbed. It became a routine for them...it was crazy!

Everyone didn't fall for X's strong arm tactics. One day he got his jaw wired for something he didn't do. All the dirt he did with his own hands nothing really happened to him. When he was accused of taking a jacket, he had a whole family jump him. That day was really ugly for X. Word went out for retaliation for X, but X called the goons off. He felt that all the times he did shit, and was never caught, he felt as though he deserved it. He just took this one and charged it to the game.

That was the time when the President of Def Jam came up to Yonkers and X was spitting for him with his jaw wired. Regardless of what you say DMX has some principles about himself.

THAT WAS THEN & THIS IS NOW

The Superior that people knew back then was the guy that would help you build your record label into a multimillion dollar empire, and also develop your artist for you. The Superior back then would also sit back and watch people and organizations rape the poor people in town and watch them get rich. He would sit back keep quiet and turn his head that was then. Now, the Superior we know is not going for that foolishness, you better come correct.

Back then I helped people and they took advantage of my work and loyalty now you're dealing with a new regime. I'm tired of all of the crap, and I'm not taking any prisoners. I'm not afraid anymore! Those who exploit people and bloodsuckers of the poor are going to be exposed.

What do I mean by that?

Well, when my eyes were pushed open and I wanted to counter attack what was going on around me. My aunt told me I should record and put the tapes and documents in a secret and secure location, and I took her advice. This was my protection if anything was to happen to me the authorities and the media will receive letters and packages in the mail. Now, I'm much wiser and I walk through life trying to improve myself as a person and I'm trying my best to keep a family with my team not just in words but by actions and deeds. I learned that it helps us when we go through problems that arise as we go through life. We try to stay unified and work together collectively; but on the other side of that some would say that we are a gang or a mob trying to mimic the Italians. My response to that would be that I don't know too many Italians; however, I learned from the government, and politicians.

There are some people that have close family ties when you see one you may see many other family members that do a lot of things together. Some may have biological connections, some may have grown up together and have a strong bond with one another. In some cases people are falsely classified as a gang. Meanwhile, the people who label you are moving in the same direction. Trust me if they want you to be guilty they can make you guilty. They will do it!

DMX knew damn well that I will ride with him to the end. I went with him through his drug habits. I had to be around to make sure that he was alright when he was smoking. I was on his side before the deal and everything. What I'm angry with him about is that when the opportunity finally presented itself for him to change his condition he did and that's wonderful, but he knew I was struggling to take care of him. Someone pulled my coat-tail one day and told me that Bully did the same thing to you that X was doing. I blamed X for that because now people were under the impression that they can use me as he did.

Everyone in town knew that I was a friend to X and I was walking him. Everyone knew I had open arms and helped many; however, on the other side of the coin people get angry with me when I say that X is a hypocrite. One of the many hypocritical things that he says on camera or in his songs is when he talks about his boys being his family, or what he would do for his boys and them, or whatever terminology he would utilize to say how he loves those close to him. I wonder how X could say all of that and still do me dirty (stop being greedy).

I listen to the radio and hear all of the preaching's, prayers and the crying, and I'm saying to myself damn I really like this dude he's a better actor than I ever imagined. The world is so spellbound that I'm looked at as the crazy one. You have many people who have jumped on X's band-wagon and he has changed their lives. They weren't into music but now they have positioned themselves and are trying to create situations and show no love to the people who really kept this thing going.

If I knew that something was going to bring harm to X, I told him not to do it, or if he asked me for music I will tell him no. I would give him some music but I have pulled back. He has gone ahead and put into people's head to hurt me to get the music, but I know some of the right people where he can't do anything to me.

When I see X on the TV preaching and carrying on deep down inside I believe he is suffering, but some of the suffering I believe comes from Karma. Yes, Karma for not taking care of your people that helped you really get there. I know he has good in him I have seen him give millions of dollars to a church and to this day I don't know where the money went (refer to Yonkers the Lost City of Hip-Hop). I knew the situation was crooked from the beginning. I have it on video where the pastor was saying that we used to go over to their church and eat chicken and all of that nonsense, which is a bold face lie (preacher pimping). I never stepped foot in there until that moment she started lying. The first time I met the pastor was when we started doing the interviews. X sat there and invested money into that scam, whereas School 12 was the place that helped him set up his music foundation and in turn he gave nothing back!

The thing with preaching is that a lot of people know that they did some bad in their life, and when they try to change their life and become a preacher I think that they are just trying to buy their way into the place that they call heaven. My question to X is how could you be cool with the people who sold you the drugs, and the person that tried to protect you from the drugs you have no love for?

X and I started clashing when I didn't smoke or drink with him. We were clashing because I didn't give him the music we created that he would take to the studio and put out an album with. Therefore I am saying to X stop being a hypocrite because you told me that was mine and to create a situation for myself with it. It's amazing all of the things he said to me when he wrote me letters from jail regarding what I should do and what he's going to do. However, the word on the street is when a dude is in jail he writes the best letters. They would say anything, and that's why women are open to whatever those guys are writing to them from jail. Remember they have all day to think about what they're going to say and how to say it. They have so much game that they can convince an innocent woman to try and sneak them some drugs into the facility. Now that's power!

The new Superior is empowering people around him and making weak links stronger. Multiplication is the key to success, but many of the camps deal with division, subtraction and fractions. A strong unit has more of a chance to be effective. The old Superior would try to be a one man band, and try to do everything himself. Now, I have a team that's wonderful.

I have a DJ on my team from Shadyville Records DJ Moeskino. We connected and started working together; and I go out to Jersey and support him, love is love. He introduced me to Treach from Naughty by Nature next thing I know one of my guys is doing an independent movie with him about Stop the Violence. I brought the news clipping to School 12 administration to show the press what we have gotten for our work; we also had children with us. The administration behaved nonchalantly as though they didn't care. Shadyville Records is a company that Eminem started for his radio shows on the internet and Sirius. Moeskino is one of his up and coming artists, we reached an agreement and now we work together and I'm getting a lot of love from out of town.

In the past I wouldn't smile and people would say what is wrong with him? On occasions I would smile but I would be hurting deep down inside. When the X thing happened for some reason it didn't bother me; However, what hurt me was when I used to see him and address him, and he would act like he didn't see me as though I wasn't there. After all of that work that I put in with him. The average person would have flipped years ago on X. If I knew what I know now I would have supported many more back then.

This situation is so serious I will reiterate for the record!!

We weren't poor we were okay or the word I will choose is limited. My mother hustled up enough money to put clothes on our back so that we can look descent, and we were well taken care of by a single mother. As time went on my mother wanted to have fun, this is what made me put the shield around me in my life, and I put the metal all around my skin. If it wasn't for my mom I wouldn't have survived everything that I have been through in Yonkers and especially what I have been through with X.

One day my mother gave me two months' rent and moved down South and left me and told me that I have to take care of myself. I didn't have anything at the time, I was going through hard times and had X and Jinx living in the house. Those were the times that we were talking about becoming really big and getting on Def Jam we had it all figured out even the acting part. That's all we talked about I was doing artist development before I actually realized what it was. I was upset with Ruff Ryders because they knew what I did for X and they should have done something for me in their company. I used to run with Swiss back then, we spent some time together; however, as time went along we separated. Maybe he thought I wanted something from him but we were boys once upon a time.

I'm always asked how come I know so many millionaires and none of them ever reached out to me? What did I do to them? My answer is always I didn't do anything to them. It's hard looking at all of these guys on TV because after a while you begin to think that maybe it was something I did or didn't do. I began to question myself. If you're weak you can become depressed and develop an inferiority complex that can stunt your growth. I took a bad situation and used it to motivate me, which is why I named my company "Most Hated." My rational was in order for those people to do what they did to me over and over again I must be the "Most Hated."

I was a team player all the way I always gave 110%. I didn't demonstrate practices of disloyalty so what was the problem. I kept on looking in the mirror and I asked myself why do I love those that don't love me? Why am I helping those that don't help me? I put my experience and talent into building myself up, and now when I'm looked at by those who did me wrong they ask me what's my problem? I tell them that I'm the product you created. I'm something you raised, and do not be mad at their creation. I'm not blaming everyone only the people who had the power to change situations and make things happen. I worked with them and they did me wrong. But as the saying goes that was then and this is now.

When I first began revealing to the public that I was writing a book about my experiences with DMX my inner circle would say that was then and this is now. I began explaining to them that back then I was strong in the music and now in 2011 I am just repositioning myself differently in the music. To elaborate on my foundation as a party promoter I refer to that as 101. It helped set the stage that propelled my career to another level. When I repositioned myself in the business some people got the impression that either I fell off or that I didn't promote anymore. Then, other dudes stepped onto the scene and made the game more exciting and competitive. At the end of the day it's all good for business. The way that I conduct myself these days is governed around respect. I respect everyone's position and authority accordingly. I respect those that put in work over the years and are still working in the business. Now, I share with the young practitioners of the hip-hop culture the importance of respect, and how far it can take you in your music career.

Back then I was all over the place as a DJ, manager, and promoter now I am a CEO I overstand the importance of staying in your lane. Picture traveling on the road to success on the hip-hop music highway; well there may be many lanes that will take you along in your journey; you must respect the road you're traveling on at that particular time in your journey, and make sure you have money for the tolls. The sooner one learns the importance of staying in the right lane the quicker one begins to grow.

Years ago I was promoting and blowing everyone's label up, now if it's not Most Hated or in affiliation with it I will deal with the situation accordingly. Currently, the concentration is on the inner circle and keeping it tight. I still have a healthy relationship with Ruff Ryders, and Power House Studios because I was there in the beginning and played a role in the foundation. I still work with VIP Record Pool they help me push artists and get music out.

I am a different man today because my eyes are wide open whereas in the past they were closed. Before I was peeping now I'm looking at the entire picture. My eyes are open to everything such as the backstabbing, deception with the intentions of stardom, girls who say they love you because of the situation.

Another jewel from the Walked the Dog playbook: ***Find a woman and tell her that you don't have shit and if she sticks with you for at least a year she is the one to be with.***

Back in the days I didn't have aspirations or even think about becoming a boss. I was a loyal soldier who could be led to his death by someone sitting in a command center giving orders. I'm not trying to be the dead sacrificed soldier.

Years ago I was on the front line for the company I was representing I gave 110%. Don't get me wrong every organization needs soldiers, captains, generals, and have a command team that is going to lead you into victory. Moreover, they will share some of the benefits of being victorious with the soldiers the ones that have sacrificed the most. At this time I lead my soldiers with a low casualty rate. I strive for no casualties. I send them out equipped so that they can come back and become lieutenants and captains of their own ship.

I teach and educate my team so they will not become victims or become destroyed mentally. I encourage all to create a plan and stick to it. Move to your own beat and never get boxed in by social norms. Social norms create restrictions on your mentality and stop you from asking questions. When you stop asking questions you stop analyzing and thinking. When you stop thinking one is truly dead.

What an artist should know from then and now is that you must have principles of loyalty within your team. Nothing should be able to break the bond.

Here's an example: I was on X's team faithfully devoted my main goal was to make sure that his music was heard and the world got a chance to see him. I invested some of my own money what little I had at the time. I utilized all of my resources and networks to get the job done. I demonstrated that action speaks louder than words mentally I was a key asset to the operation.

Another jewel from the Walk the Dog playbook: ***Strive to become a valuable asset in any business or***

organization that you become involved in. Specialize or master something. If you're going to be somebody's flunky become a flunky with a goal in mind. Utilize education, technology, and common sense.

When you're an asset it's a little easier to become connected with another organization and set up another situation. If one is ever blessed to have a person like that in your circle make sure you take care of him/her. That’s the person that you are going to keep close to you.

I was that person in the DMX scenario who was lost in the shuffle. While I was surrounded by people with the poker face they were dealing from the bottom of the deck. After I played the hand that I was dealt I had to smarten up because if you're not strong the industry can and will play a number on you. It can turn loved ones against you then spit you out. Once I saw with my own eyes what the industry will do. I knew that it wasn't just limited to hip-hop. I'm sure that those destructive elements are in all of the major institutions of power.

That's why I am spreading awareness in these days and times because I'm worried if you speak your mind you will be labeled as a terrorist. I'm not trying to become that in the music industry. The old word used to be nigger now that word bounces off some people like rubber bouncing off a pavement. In the new world it is going to be terrorist it went from nigger to terrorist. The place that I'm from I don't know if it's Willie Lynch, ignorance, selfishness, or the infamous "black cloud."

Collectively if we weren't divided we could do really big things. Why is everyone walking on eggshells? Why doesn't anyone really want to help the next man? If someone feels as though you are coming to fill their spot they will do anything in their power to prevent it; never looking at how the next man can improve their position.

Let's examine the rap scene what happened back then is happening now, you have a bunch of groups on a label that will never come out. There maybe one or two people who will shine and that's it. You can refer to the 48 power of law. When you keep a person wanting and needing they are going to be loyal why not set it up where everyone can eat, and the powers that be can eat more.

There is a black cloud around Yonkers it's almost impossible to get around because the residue is so thick. It almost had me but I survived it I think it gave up on me. It said I can't break him and it was going to move on but it is still here. For years there have been rumors of the black cloud in Yonkers. Some say it's a myth while others swear by it. Personally I think the black cloud was manmade. I know several people whose wicked actions and demonic spirits feed the cloud.

They are saying that there is no money in the rap game and that's a lie. You can still sell 100,000 independently and become a millionaire, but they don't want you to know that. Have you ever seen anyone getting out of the shower and you can see the steam coming off their body; steam goes up into the sky. There are beings in Yonkers through hate, envy, and greed is generating energy that poisons the atmosphere and creates what is termed the black cloud.

I teach new people in the industry that you don't necessarily have to give back with money you can give back by giving a person an opportunity. Some may deny its existence but their actions will prove them wrong as well. The black cloud manifests and takes different forms. The question may arise what did Superior do so badly to DMX? My answer is the black cloud. Most people that live here will recognize the existence of such a negative force but depending on what click they are in they may downplay the power of its existence. There are some who are in denial and let's not forget some of the people that are in power feed the black cloud and use it to their advantage. Just make a simple observation and you will quickly see how full of shit some people really are. That's the point that I'm trying to drive home to the reader. How a community can and will destroy you, use you for all that they can use you for and spit you out. Please overstand that I poured my heart out. I have done some things that I'm not proud of as well, but I changed my life and did what society said to do to be a so-called good person. Can I get the word of god from the pastor without giving up all of my money?

I was loyal to a team of guys with a goal in mind. It was the hand I was dealt, it's what the streets offered me. What did the streets offer me? They offered me the Tribal Brothers so I went along with it, and from the outside it looked good. We had issues though like any other family. The leader was too head strong and flashy and all about him. What I got out of that was you need to be your own man. The streets offered me DJ Kasun and what did I get from that? I learned how to step my DJ game up and how to make some money. He was a money maker and what he was doing with X rubbed off on me. I met X through him and when he went to jail I carried on the torch. I kept DMX's name out, but when DMX got his first break-through look what happened. He got his first single out on Def Jam "Get at Me Dog" and it blew up and I got no love. I was working day and night even while he was in jail I was holding it down. He was like do this for me, and do that for me we are going to do this and that we're a team. But did he keep his word?

Ruff Ryders was a group of guys from the streets that came together. I appreciated the fact that they came from another town and recognized the talent that was in Yonkers. My issue was they didn't take care of the people who held them down when they came to town. That was a slap in the face!

Society always talks about doing the right thing helping others but what does it get you? Hurt and anger. I'm happy I recorded my experiences and dealings with X. If I didn't I would have had nothing if I would have left it to someone else to recognize my work. Whoever has access to the media paints the picture and tells their story.

By observing the chain of events that took place with the music in my town I see how history can become distorted easily! Money and opportunists can alter true accounts of events. They can tie themselves into history. It's done all of the time. The only reason why they can't completely eliminate my contributions is because I have the most footage of DMX in the world. Ask the powers that be how I was able to get that much material if my role was not significant. Building a star is not easy it takes focus, sacrifice and dedication. Those are the principles that can get you through obstacles that can arise in the pursuit of your long term goals. Artists must remain connected to their core values.

DMX and I will always have a certain level of love for one another; but I think that he has a deep embedded animosity against me because I will not hand over to him certain important materials. Previously, I would have given him anything that I had, but he didn't respect me or protect me, instead he fed me to the sharks. Now when I contact my lawyer and I want a percentage of the proceeds of any materials that is being produced now we have a problem. The game is crazy when you wake up and want to do business you're a problem. Now, I look like the enemy. I live by that old saying education is expensive but ignorance will cost you more.

WORK ETHIC

They say music calms the savage beast well I beg to differ. I say music can also activate the savage beast and make people behave and respond in some very interesting ways. Nearly everyone knows or acknowledges that music has some type of effect on the listener. At the office, the music that is played is usually calm and motivating.

Classical, Reggae, Country and Hip-hop music can have a different effect on people, and heavy metal tones, vibrations and frequencies also affects people differently who are consuming the sound. Receiving a massage is soothing and quiet; therefore, the music there is designed to have a relaxing therapeutic effect. Many people have never done a deep study into the effects of music and the human brain or behavior. But, growing up in music and being surrounded by it all my life, I just knew there had to be a coalition. However, I couldn't explain it when I was younger. But I always wondered why my aunt will always start crying when she hears a certain song come on. Now it makes sense and it's the same with hip hop. Sometimes you can play a certain record and the beat will just do something to people. I knew it was the music.

As I became more sophisticated in my studies it lead me to the branch of science called the cognitive neuroscience of music, a branch of science that studies the effect of music in the behavior of humans and animals. They have found in their studies that different pitches in music have different effects in the brain from low to very high pitches that send frequencies that alter moods in people. Scientist also found that people who have some music training have the ability to memorize a little more than someone who was not formally trained in music. Many debates may arise about music especially when you consider whether or not learning actually takes place. Most researchers are in agreement that studying music leads to positive development of the human brain. In 1991 French Reservist Alfred A. Tomatis in his book "Why Mozart" attempted to utilize Mozart's music to prove his belief that music stimulates the brain and promotes healing. He coined it the "Mozart Effect."

Is becoming a great rapper, producer, and artist only about having the ability to create songs or put words together? Or is it about being able to play instruments and create wonderful melodies?

We all know or have seen some really talented individuals on stage that are not a household name. Some are talented but are lazy and unreliable. Some are exceptionally talented; however their ego gets in the way. While others have it and think that it's just going to come to them.

Why do most never make it while others soar?

In this chapter we are going to examine DMX's work ethic which we call the work ethic of superstars.

In the beginning I didn't understand DMX's work ethic, as an artist his method was weird to me. In the beginning he wouldn't let me see him write. There were times that he never wrote in front of me. A lot of times I didn't know what he was bringing to the table. I learned that while we were making mixed tapes he would sit around all day listening to his music over and over again all day until he was able to master it. His objective was to be able to do any song in any manner, style or beat. He's a lyrical beast not only with his lyrics also with his flow, and his delivery.

In my experience in the game I have seen a lot of MC's write something and say I wrote that to this beat, but I'm not able to use it for that beat. X didn't write like that he would just switch his flow up and move a different way and we all knew that he would be singing the rhymes as well. That's entirely another level! If you examine some of the other great hip hop legends you see that most share the same work ethic that make them great. X also had this big rhyme bible or big book that he had all his rhymes in. He would keep writing until he filled the book up. I don't know how many rhymes are in those books, but I remember him saying that one day one of these books is going to make millions of dollars. He didn't lie about that. His work ethic and the approach that he takes is not the norm. He would spend time on mastering his flow and what to say to make the crowd go crazy without it being so complicated. He writes like he's talking to you only the great ones have that ability. Just pay attention most MC's don't do that. It didn't matter if he was getting high he had a book right there with him writing. If he was with a female he was writing about it, he was always writing.

FLYER

Here is a jewel from DMX that will probably help an MC step his game up a little: ***X always told me to write like someone is standing in front of you and you want to destroy him with your lyrics. Word play and delivery your lyrics have to be creative and you always have to be prepared.***

No other rapper will ever compare to X because when most get into the game they get in for different reasons. Through all of our conversations he never said that he wanted to get into the game because he wanted to buy this or that, do this or that. It wasn't for cars, jewelry or women that was never his thing. He worked the craft, he learned the tools of the craft and perfected them and in turn it made him a better lyricist. I teach those that listen to me the importance of learning and perfecting the craft. Artists have 2 albums or 2 songs and think that they have perfected the craft. I think his other motivation was to show his mother that he can do well without her.

Most MC's don't have their heart in it and if they do it's for a moment or the money. DMX never really cared about the money because his quality stayed the same broke, or with money. He's like a factory usually when one is comfortable they get slack and that's the difference between DMX and another MC.

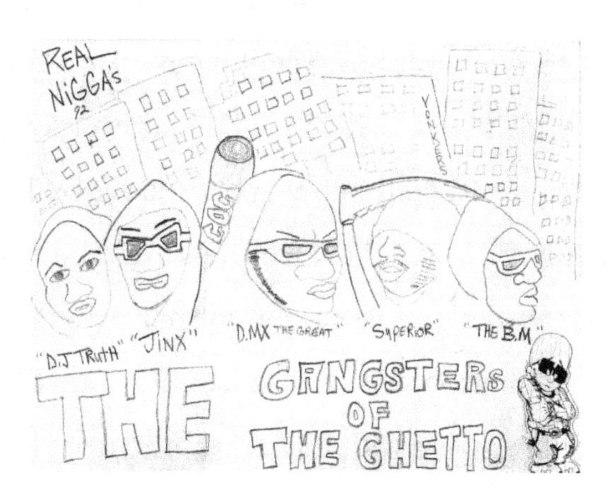

GANGSTERS OF THE GHETTO (G.O.G) FLYER

There are many rappers who battle and talk shit from afar, or on record and radio but X will bring it to your face. Don't forget he battled Jay-Z face to face. If you ask me I think that battle was a tie because Jay was really kicking that street shit and that money shit. I wish you would have heard what Jay was kicking. X is more of a darker rapper. He was talking about robbing him and the rich executives making money. Both of them kept going, guns were pulled out on both sides because Ruff Ryders were not backing down and neither was Roc-a-Fella. That day was crazy!

K-Solo lost the battle that they had in jail; later on Solo said that X stole his Spellbound. He said that he came out with it first with EPMD, and everyone knows that's not true. We all know about the DMX-Bill Blass battle; and back in the days we tried to get him to battle Lord Finesse, but for some reason that didn't work out. Whatever the reason was, X is so confident that he would go up against anyone with no fear at any time.

X can produce strong lyrics in different categories and subject matter, which also separates him from most.

When you talk about work ethic and comparing him to others I can say that he may have the ability to write the rhymes and develop his craft; but as far as putting together in song format he may not have that ability and that's where I come in to play. As far as writing, lyrics and producing songs I have to say Tupac was on top of his game. Both of them can make you cry and make you angry with them...one will say dear mama, and the other will say fuck my mama. They share a lot of similar traits but are different in many ways.

X can get a little scary for some people for example he will start saying things such as the devil took his soul, and rapping and having conversations with Damien seems more real than just entertainment. I reflect back on when he would be around looking at people and his presence would give people the creeps. Many people said that they would get bad vibes from him. He was really 2 different people. An older person said to me one day who really wants to have a conversation with Damien? However, for some strange reason I was never afraid of him or afraid to be around him. He never did any of the things to me that he did to other people. I wasn't afraid because I think I balanced him out. He wouldn't let me do any crazy shit, he would say let me do it. If anything came up that he got into trouble for he would come to me and I would fix it.

These days I see most rapper's trying their best to create good hooks and the verses are garbage. They are another type of breed unlike the older rappers who appreciate the craft. I guess that's why it was so hard to get into the game because they had to come with something. Since the music industry is changing and will never return to the way things used to be anyone can put anything out. If you want the quality of hip-hop to return we must start creating and breeding worthy lyrics and lyricists, and eventually the quality will come back to the culture. There are too many distractions these days as soon as a rapper has one hit he's starting a record label and instantly becomes a businessman. Having too many tasks people do not take you seriously plus your concentration will be divided.

X was always focused. He was always walking the dog, and the dog he was walking always stayed hungry. Therefore, we kept the dog fed, healthy, gave it plenty of exercise, and then the dog grew up! The dog went around the world biting mutts taking them down by the necks. That's just one way we walked the dog. DMX is operating on that level his work ethic is just incredible. Think about when he was putting albums out in the early 2000's, he was doing a movie every year to go along with it. I would really like the reader to think for a moment about all of the energy and effort that it took to do that. Think about it long days on a set, and long nights in the studio.

DMX Film Facts (a few):

1999 - He played a leading role in Belly

2000 - Romeo Must Die

2001 - Exit Wounds

2003 - Cradle to the Grave

2004 - Never Die Alone

That's what I would consider high grade work ethic. I remember conversations that we had in my house about music and silver screen then I see him on there with Steven Segal, Eva Mendez, Jet Li, and Tom Arnold. I wish I was able to meet Anthony Anderson he looks as though he's a good person to be around with on the set.

I would like to thank DMX for bringing Aaliyah to Yonkers when they did the video "Romeo must Die." They set up shop in Mulford Gardens, and X brought Aaliyah to the projects and it was all good because she was with a dog. I will never forget that for the rest of my life. That's the body of work that will be here through the ages. A lot of these up and coming artists don't have their heart in the game, connoisseurs in the music game can see it. Most new artists if you look at their work line by line lyrically it is questionable, and very few have stage presence.

Have you ever been to a DMX concert? Or have you ever seen him on stage? He is a good example of how you are supposed to work the stage and the crowd.

Here's a precious jewel from the Walk the Dog playbook: ***As you develop your flow and word play develop your stage presence it's your connection to your audience. Good stage presence will take you a long way!***

Another jewel from the Walk the Dog playbook: ***As a new artist or spring chicken so to speak bring something new to the game.***

Over the last couple of years as I watched rappers go on interviews most of them have the same lullaby, which is "Yo, I have been rapping since I was 4 years old, I lost my father at a young age, I never knew my father, or I'm starting my own company." When we were "Walking the Dog" we didn't care about any of that. Our main concern was how we had to rip others words apart and simply rip it. In the lab where we laid all of the music down I had many pictures of different rappers on the wall. The pictures were motivation to get onto Def Jam because it seemed as though we were forgetting the biggest label around. Plus it was motivation for DMX who was writing rhymes about all of the rappers that were on the wall just in case we encountered them on the streets.

One of the top artists on the wall at the time and of the past was EPMD, LL Cool J, Rakhim, and Big Daddy Kane. Basically, everyone in the industry we had material for them and material that would get us noticed by them, which was our goal. We weren't trying to disrespect them we wanted to let them know that we wanted to be next to them. The pictures on the wall were for inspiration. Mulford Gardens was a hip-hop training camp where younger artists like Jinx would sit around watch, and learn from us. From this experience came Marlon from the group Sporty Thievz (R.I.P.) who was with us in the beginning.

The formula that we used in our training camp is designed (if utilized properly) to breed a superior lyricist, much greater than the average M.C. When they are of a certain bloodline and have natural talent this formula immediately upgrades, re-boot and re-configures, and they are equipped with the ability to flow on another level. This is the foundation for a good work ethic, but there are also other elements that determine the level of success just keep that in mind.

When X is in the booth he is a beast. He likes to run right through it. Most of the time he gets it in one take. I can't recall him being in the booth for long periods of time. He's not the type of artist who becomes frustrated in the booth, can't get to lay it like they want, take a break, and come back to it. No, he gets it in one take. For X that's his signature! He got to a point where he was knocking out five songs a day. When I say songs I mean real songs not like what they are doing today, where you have a long hook, a verse, and a hook. Years ago we were taking other people's songs and doing our version to it, that's an old practice. X came way before his time.

As people look at him now and see him in trouble all the time their main question is what's the problem? What they do not know is that is how he has always been; and the difference is that back then he had a good team around him who made sure that the public didn't see his chaos. It was a cover up, but now that the sheets are off people want to act surprised like this is new. But his behavior doesn't surprise me I know that he has been like that all along.

When you take the time to think about it, all of the trouble that X goes through in his personal life, he still has a better body of work than most artists.

FLYERS

That says a lot because those so called artists that are supposed to have their shit together and have a sober mind can't really say the same.

I ask myself, how can I go through what that man has been through all of his life and still manage to rise to the top?

People ask me why he is always getting arrested. All I tell them is that he was getting arrested regularly before he ever had a record deal. He had a record before he had a record deal. His rap sheet was long before the world heard of a DMX. What caught the attention of the masses was his talent and work ethic. At the time when I was developing X I went in knowing that we weren't building an artist we were developing a superstar. The Ruff Ryders at the time were building a movement, but they had no one to carry the flag and that is where X came in, he was a man that wasn't seeking fame or fortune. X was in the game just to be in ciphers and get his music heard, and get some recognition.

Like the day he was in cipher with Mobb Deep and X was trying to give it to them. Also, when Snoop Dogg and Death Row came to Yonkers and wanted to sign X, I was sitting up there with Snoop and Corrupt and the rest of them and they were all flowing. However, X was there on some other stuff. The average rapper would have been overwhelmed by the pressure, but X didn't give a damn. Everything was a battle I remember that day when X was kicking his rhymes he was getting at them. He said "New York Nigga's don't fuck with perms." I was thinking this kid is bugging. I don't know how Snoop and his crew took it that night, but I was waiting for something to pop off. He didn't care about money he was just rapping. He wasn't thinking about business until people started getting into his ear saying that your people are robbing you. That's the average artist's mentality. The average artist doesn't want to do any work until they feel they are getting robbed or money is being embezzled from them, then all of a sudden they have work ethics.

Now that they are businessmen or calling themselves a businessman they still need to have a proper work ethic, and that's what I brought to the table when I Walked the Dog. At the end of the day it's sad to say that you can work for the average organization or corporation and bust your ass for them for years, you think that you're going to be rewarded, and remembered but in essence you're not. It's sad but true. The name of the game is doing what you have to do so that you can get ahead and don't worry about stepping on anyone to get there. That's the American Way!!

I have seen artists do a song and disappear and will not record again for weeks. I have seen some write one day and skip two days and write another two days then take another week off; but I have never seen anyone with the issues that X has with drugs and the streets I'm talking about being really heavy in the streets and still write and record every day.

THE KENNEL

The kennel aka the breeding group aka my camp record label or new pups that I'm walking. I call them pups out of respect. Some are still young and need plenty of nurturing and care. Many of them didn't get all of their shots as of yet. So I keep them close to me and pumped up with the formula.

This formula is special. It's the same formula I fed the prized dogs of a special bloodline. The ingredients have been sought after ever since DMX left the dog house. Some tried to strong arm me, some tried to put some females on me to seduce me out of it, and it even came down to espionage. They surrounded me with spies and double agents in search of the formula that I won't reveal as of yet. Let's not forget the key to having loyal dogs in the kennel is respect; you don't have to give hot sauce or chain them up you just need to respect the dogs. It's more than just a bark. They are there to provide a service.

I always took into consideration when raising a breed of pups it is the genetic qualities and make up especially for breeding purposes. Therefore, I say for the record, the bloodline of my breed has no defects. I realized with young pups getting them trained is the first priority. I make sure I keep them clean and free of infection and diseases. A breeder of my experience can see defects and illness. I'm more concerned with teeth, head shapes, and bone structure. Those are some of the fundamentals for good stock; whereas, that type of knowledge comes in handy when it's training time. Please let's not forget the financial commitment and annual cost such as food and grooming supplies.

In a puppy's early development you can see what they are made of you can usually read if they are submissive, dominant, fearful or aggressive. I don't know about other people, but for myself, I don't take in every dog that comes to me wagging its tail, which I learned from my experiences. They may be friendly dogs at times, but could have issues such as diseases or fleas.

Subsequently, one of the many secrets in raising puppies is how you live and interact with you pups is the foundation for an excellent long term relationship.

Now-a-days, the pups that I am walking are easy to potty train to use the bathroom on the newspaper. So it's going to be easier to get them to get the training they need to make them possible grand champs. First let me talk about the female pups that I am walking. The female pups require special treatment. Female pups will always take care of you and protect you; however, you have to keep an eye on them! A real strong pup in my kennel is a female named Yvonne who is a triple threat. She sings, raps, and acts. She is even a song writer and does Broadway shows. She is an educator and I consider her a blue nose pit.

Yvonne McFall:

E.V. Mac in one word would say that she is versatile, while many others describe her as a double - triple threat. Not only is she a singer, but she is also an actress, dancer, teacher, song-writer, and T.V. and radio show host. She began her artistic journey at the age of 6 through the gift of voice, everything that came afterwards was considered to be her sense of artistic development.

Presently, she represents the R&B female side of Most Hated Entertainment established by CEO Superior. Superior produced her first mixed CD and DVD entitled, "Thoughts of a Single Black Woman," and "Voices from the Heart," an R&B compilation. She met Superior six years ago. Not only is he her manager, but also a great friend. Through Most Hated, Superior has created a family of brotherhood and true threats. DMX set the path and she only hopes to create new ones, which Superior will be proud of as well. If you ask EV how she feels about the CEO she would say, "He is a man unlike any other, with a heart beyond life itself. He is loyal, dedicated, diligent, honest, and if you have the pleasure of crossing paths with him, thank God above because Superior is truly a unique blessing."

Pearls or Purly Wyte was hanging around the Yonkers streets trying to get on. She was considered a stray pup. I was also told by a few dog catchers that she could be also seen trying to get a meal on D-Block. It was said that they would pet her (give her advice, but would never feed her). As soon as they found out she was in my kennel, they started to advise her of what to do, and what not to do.

They still weren't feeding her but they let her smell and look at the food. There are a lot of dying dogs around town. I tried to call the organization P.E.T.A. a couple of times to get some help for them, because no one loved these dogs around here, until they found out that Superior has them in his camp or that he put a collar on the pup and became their caretaker. Now everyone is a dog-lover, or at least now have interest in dogs in distress.

Purly Wyte:

Superior is my manager. He has a vision for Most Hated Entertainment and he is determined to help all of his artists reach their goals. Although a mass amount of people trying to throw salt on the movement, he still sticks by our side and gives us advice to better ourselves. I am the newest relevant member of Most Hated

Entertainment, and I know in my heart that God teamed me up with Superior for great reasons.

Mixed ladies, I call them pups but they are not full breed because they are different. They are not from the artist bloodline. They are very supportive and instrumental in getting the group out there. Over time and through experience I have learned to appreciate their bloodline also. They are what I call showroom pits and they are not vicious or fighters. They are the ones that people like to look at. As a group they have become close and supportive of each other in business and promotional ventures they are real tight and roll in packs. I have the utmost respect for them. A lot of people own dogs, but they are taken care of by their trainers.

Rowdy City- I consider them to be strong pits from a good bloodline with a lot of potential from Connecticut. Right now, I got them training real hard in the formula. I expect to see great things from them in the near future.

ROWDY CITY
(MOSTHATED/CONNECTICUT)

Rowdy City:

We met Superior as youth's in Yonkers, NY while we were living in projects of "Mulford Gardens." It was there we had developed a big brother/little brother relationship. I was a young boy on the streets getting caught up in the life. I was always talented at basketball; Superior saw that and would let me focus on anything else. Having him there to help keep me focused I eventually moved in the right direction and went off to school on a full basketball scholarship to the University of Bridgeport. I always wanted to show Superior that

I've been writing lyrics, but I was afraid to reveal myself before I felt I was good enough.

I eventually came to him and was like "Yo Bruh, I know I'm nice in ball, but I'm nice with this rap shit too." In the beginning he wasn't trying to hear it, but then some young cats were at School 12 battling and free styling so I jumped in. I believe it was that moment that impressed him enough to say I was ready to take the next step. He then told me to establish a group and a following up in Connecticut. He always had a great vision for expansion; he looked at CT as another place for Most Hated to conquer. That was the very birth of "Rowdy City." He always coached me up to be the better and more prepared MC. He always said things like "Always be ready for whatever….Have 10- 16's in your head to battle anyone! When you are in front of the crowd, make them feel Most Hated throughout the entire building.

The best things that I have to say about Superior are away from the music. He has always been like a father figure in my life, and throughout many lives in the

Yonkers Community. To many he was the first to help them get a job, education, scholarships, etc. He is a true ambassador for the City of Yonkers in a major way!

He always told me and reminded me that Most Hated would stand for people who were against all odds, no support system, and still able to find the will power within to become successful! That is what Most Hated is about, that is what Superior is about. To this day those words of encouragement have stuck in my head, and I know for a fact he will not let me fail. He will not let Most Hated Fail. After all we are all one family.

DOUBLE BARREL
(MOSTHATED YONKERS)

Double Barrel:

They are two strong Pitts with attitudes of Bull Masters. They are extremely talented brothers and they are twins. They produce and rap and when I let them off the chain it's going to be lots of problems.

S.K.I.T.S
(STAND FIRM/MOSTHATED BX)

Skits:

A strong pit from the Bronx what I like about him is that he is a real loyal pit. He is a dog that will never let anyone get near or touch the master. Plus he is extremely talented and driven.

DJ Moeskino- is one of my prized pits that found his way from New Jersey into my kennel. He is healthy and from a good bloodline the type of pit that dog lovers will love to breed. Even though he is down with Eminem and the shady dale DJ's camp, I see it like this. Moeskino is a prize dog who has a rich owner but the rich owner doesn't have time to raise, nurture, and spend time with him. That's where I come in. Now I got him in my camp on the formula.

Moeskino:

What's up this is G-Units, Shadyville DJ Moeskino the official DJ for Most Hated Records & NBA Tim Thomas (Nutzo) Official DJ. Myself and Superior put a lot of planning and work in together to make things actually happen within the movement. Superior is a made-man; he's a boss, a good brother and a soldier who fights for everything he believes in. Most importantly he's overdue to have his day. The streets as well as the industry need to know his story/history with the Dog Dark Man X…..

Tray Dot- She is also a blue nose female feisty pit. Most female dogs can be petted, but not this one. I've see her on several occasions trying to bite the hands of people trying to pet her. Her rap style is strong and hardcore. Use caution, beware of this dog.

Bully- I mention him because he was raised in my kennel. I gave him some formula when he was young. He is a big strong dog now who happened to pop his chain, got away and ran into the streets. There are a lot of dog catchers out there trying to claim rights to him.

Some even say they have papers on him and tried to put a collar on him. That's alright! But all dog owners know that a lost dog will eventually find his way home.

I don't consider him a pit. I would say he is a bull dog/Doberman pitcher. If you raise a Doberman right, they say that particular dog will never cross you. But every now and then it has been recorded that some Dobermans turned and even killed some of their masters if they don't receive the right attention and with that in mind I keep some vets close to me just in case I have to put some of my dogs to sleep. That's a real emotional burdened on any dog owner or lover. When they too have to make decisions I always say, to help with the grief, get another puppy before you put the old or sick dog to sleep. It helps ease the pain and help you to deal with the loss a little better.

We have been staying really busy for the last couple of years. We open up for Lloyd Banks twice up in Connecticut. We opened up for Omarion in Pennsylvania and even for the comedian Michael Blackstone better known for his role in Ice cube's Friday movie. We recently did some work for Dip Set, Jim Jones, Jules Santana, and Cam'ron when they all performed in Connecticut. We also opened up for Mills from Young Money and clips in White Plains and DMX before he was sent to jail. The kennel has been putting in a lot of work or what I call dog shows. I brought my pups around other pups to interact and also get a chance to showcase my dogs with some other prize pups.

DRUGS ENTERTAINMENT & HIP-HOP

Growing up in a Yonkers housing Project truly prepared me for what the world had to offer like love, hate, sex, violence and drugs. I guess when you are a child you really don't see the effects of drugs on people or the long term effects it has on the community.

I remember playing in Grant Park and while we were playing and having fun, there would be some older guns over in the corner shooting dice. I remember the loud music, laughing, and sometimes yelling and the funny aroma that would periodically pass my nostrils in, which was brought to my attention that it was the smell of marijuana, as time passed the smell became part of the environment. I smelled it when I was playing in the park, every day. It was there just like the leaves, the flowers, the basketball court, swings, and monkey bars we were just told to stay away from it. But I was young, naive and innocent at the time. Then eventually my eyes were popped wide open and my innocence disappeared with the introduction of crack to the hood.

The older guys in the hood used to play a song by Melle-Mell called White Lines and it was talking about cocaine and base; but I never saw any evidence of that around because people who used cocaine didn't use it in public like those who smoked marijuana; however, crack changed the dynamics of society.

With the introduction of crack I saw powerful, established, and respectable people turn into the worse base heads you can imagine and crack was the equalizer.

It was like a civilian in a war-zone and the causalities were all round me. My innocence was gone never to return. I used to look out my window and see the children playing and watch the adults socializing, mixed with the sounds of music and laughter.

Now, I was looking out of the window and I didn't see as many children playing as I saw in the past. Now when I saw the adults I noticed the difference but I couldn't put my finger on it at the time. So I started asking questions such as why is everyone going in and out of building "24."

Why are some people carrying televisions and VCR's into the building and not coming back out with them? Why are so many people all of a sudden getting robbed for jewelry? Why are so many people's apartments getting robbed?

The answer that was given to me was crack and I was introduced to another word and it was called base head or crack head. Most people just see this character on TV or in the movies but I have seen this character live and in action. Movie scripts have nothing on what I saw in the projects of Yonkers creating despair for some, and opportunity for others. Base heads will sell all of the food out of their refrigerator to get a hit. Their children and families can almost starve to death, until the same drug dealer provided food to the same female crack head for sexual exploitation.

How do you think this affected the children of this time?

When the dealer started to see how much power of the drug they had, they would do anything imaginable for a hit of crack. I even saw some dealers make a joke out of a crack head getting naked and humping a tree as if he was having sex all for the laughs of course. The thing that caught my attention that was crack related was in Mary J. Blige's old projects when they made this woman have sex with a pit-bull for some crack. After you see something like that you would never be the same. How can you be?

I remember when public enemy came out with the song "night of the living base heads." I was like oh shit. It's everywhere and spreading quickly across the country. It was surprising to me at the time because I was just boxed in the hood and that's all I knew because I never left the hood. I based everything off of what was learned in the hood, therefore I couldn't think outside of that box. But one thing I knew was that if the kids were making money in my hood from selling drugs, money was being made in the ghettos around the country.

It was once said to me that banks and creditors were not loaning any money to low income blacks. With that being said crack was a way that people in the hood could come up and eat, selling cocaine crack in plastic bottles with black, blue and red tops.

Years later I realized the drug infested environment that I grew up in prepared me for the world. As I got older, I realized that drug dealers wear suits and ties and many were well educated. When I finally got involved in the music, I was trained and well prepared to deal with those slime balls.

In the music and entertainment business I always knew drugs were around, I just didn't know how it was operating, but I knew it wouldn't take too long to show its ugly face. So I sat back and watched and I realized that some people came in the industry drug addicts, and you had some that came in squeaky clean, but the stress and the pressure of the business led them to drugs.

I know of some that had deadlines for albums and needed something to keep them all night so that they could record. Then you had some that needed something to help them go to sleep and they found that something that helped them. Now, as I talk to other producers and

CEO's around the country there have been several conversations about how younger artists feel. They say they feel as though they can't even go into the studio without having a blunt or a shot of something. Some artists argue that their particular stimulant gives them a creative edge.

In the entertainment industry, one of the key principles that are utilized is the principle of exploitation. One thing you can put your money on is that if there is a talented artist out there with superstar potential and he/she happens to be on drugs; trust me the think tank for that label will devise a plan to exploit that particular artist to make as much money from him/her as they can before they become burnt out.

Subsequently, the question often arises well how about X? And my answer is DMX was nice before the drugs or the hard drugs. He was so nice, he was just rapping as a sport.

He was literally on some other shit. Most of the industry people at the time couldn't get a gauge on him. His music was incredible, but they had to use caution.

When I lecture to the young people and I'm asked about DMX and drugs I take them back to a real life changing time that affected my friend until this day, and that is when DMX was smoking Marijuana with this individual. The individual wasn't only smoking marijuana but also had a blunt that had some marijuana and crack cocaine in it. A Street term for it is to say that "the weed was laced." That day was the changing point in his life. Years later it was told to me by an older guy that there is always someone at the bar trying to slip something in someone's drink. Now-a-days some call it the date-rape drug. They say if you're in a club and you walk away from your drink, and come back to it, and it's still there unattended, you should purchase another one. These are some things that should be discussed with our youth so they can be properly prepared in this world of predators and slime balls.

What X and I discussed that day he told me what had happened to him. It was so deep that I won't even put it in the book out of respect for my dog and our friendship. This was before the music awards, and platinum albums.

When "Get at me Dog" hit the streets there was a big bidding war for DMX. I remember we had a meeting with Bad Boy Diddy wanted X on the roster with Biggie. The Lox were already signed for Bad Boys. X came into the building ready to rob and steal. His mentality was these are the nigga's making the money off of selling records drinking champagne, and driving foreign cars. Well, these are the nigga's I'm going to rob then; that day, Diddy got caught slipping and X walked away with his Rolex.

When it all went down, the dog came in hungry and "Stop being Greedy" was out, and that's how he was living at the time. What caught my attention was how calm Diddy was and he said "That's a million dollar crack head." That's how DMX was going through the industry. There were no royalty checks coming in at the time now instead of robbing people in the streets now he can rob some industry executives and artists, who he considered dog food, easy prey.

X is the type of Dog whatever position he is in he always has a sense of control. Sometimes I don't know if it was the drugs the streets or his don't give a fuck attitude. At the peak of the bidding war Shuge Knight sent the dog pound to town. That's when I first met Corrupt. We were in a studio and they had a cipher going on. Then X started to spit. Sometimes in ciphers all the rappers will be kicking the flows and everything will be on the up and up. Even though everyone will be saying that they are the best and no other rapper can do what they can do. Then you have some ciphers where rappers would be flowing back and forth and someone in the cipher would start saying slick shit out of the mouth or coming at another rapper directly or indirectly. If you know X, you know that he was relentless for doing that. We're in the cipher with the dog pound and X started saying things about the West Coast. I was giving him that look like chill out man the money is here, but he kept going. Then he would say lyrics like East Coast nigga's don't where no perms. I looked at Snoop and said X don't fuck up again always trying to take a rapper down lyrically. I know Snoop peeped it out, but he was on some cool out shit and just wanted to get to the strip club.

As I look back on it now maybe that's why Snoop and DMX never collaborated on a song in the past throughout the years. Snoop probably didn't want to fuck with him after that based on the principle of respect. It was clear that they were different type of dogs.

The industry was just a new playground for the dog. Money, sex and drugs, all were easily accessible. With that in mind, he spent the whole 1st promo tour we had robbing executives, artist, and fans. One day we were promoting the first album and a fan came up with some jewelry and was saying DMX I love your music man, I'm a big fan he said to him. DMX replied, "Thanks I like your chain," and the guy started telling him how much it cost and where he got it from. X was like cool. Then X said, let me try it on and see how it looks on me. Then the dude took the chain off his neck and placed it around X's neck. And what he didn't know was that I knew he wasn't getting it back. After X got the chain, he said good looking money then X started walking with a group of Ruff Ryder's and the dude started walking with the crew not knowing he had just been robbed from X. He was following us for a while trying to get X's attention and at the same time being careful of not pissing off any of the goons from the crew. X saw the dude following him so he eventually jumped on a motorcycle and disappeared with the chain. That's how easy it was.

Some people get into the entertainment business seeking fame and fortune and will do practically anything for the opportunities X had. When the subject of his opportunities came up, people have a hard time comprehending that he really didn't give a damn.

Some critics say that if X wasn't a drug addict then he could have been one of the greatest and that his drug use made executives second guess signing him to any big deals. It was said that investments in him are risky. I would just smile and keep my mouth shut and just hear them out. So I took a look at the history of some of the greatest groups of all times and discovered the same problems with illegal drugs and prescription drugs.

I started researching **The Beetles**, and their use of the drug Benzedrine which is a stimulant that is inhaled and is very addictive, and it is also recorded that Paul liked weed, Ringo loved booze & heroin, for John and George the drug of choice was cocaine at the time. (Refer to John Lennon 1967 Anthology).

In 1969 Elvis was staying at the international hotel in Las Vegas while doing shows in which it is said he used amphetamines before the show and tranquilizers after. Then in 1973 Elvis overdosed twice on Barbiturates and by the end of the year he was admitted into the Baptist Hospital in Memphis Tennessee. It is said that when Elvis was in the hospital his road manager and Dr. Nick searched his bedroom at Graceland and found 3 giant pharmacy jars each containing 1000's of Barbiturates, Amphetamines, and tranquilizers and he even had pills hidden in the seams of his curtains. It is said that Elvis could get a prescription from almost any doctor he visited. It is said that in 1977 Elvis had 199 prescriptions totaling more than 10,000 doses of sedatives, amphetamines, and narcotics. (Refer to Elvis Presley, the real story on his drug abuse).

Elton John:

In a book written by Elizabeth J. Rosenthal called "His Sons," she writes about Elton John's cocaine use starting in 1978 and his marijuana use to his eventual check into a rehab in 1990. Then on Jan 2nd 2010 he was reported by pop entertainment/wine services that Elton John was helping rapper Eminem for at least a month with his drug problems. Eminem told vibe magazine that he was taking as many as 20 Vicodin, Ambien, and Valium a day.

Johnny Cash:

Is said to have been addicted to amphetamines and barbiturates and it is said in Wikipedia that "Cash claims to have tried every drug there was to try."

Bob Marley:

Some say Marley wasn't a drug addict. Smoking marijuana is actually a custom in his culture as a

Rastafarian. Some argue that it aides one in the practice of meditation. Marley and the Wailers all went to jail for the use of marijuana and took a proactive vocal public position in favor of marijuana.

My research of drugs music and entertainment took me across all music genres races and age groups. I have come to the conclusion that no social circle is immune from the plague of drugs. It's just that those that choose to use drugs in the entertainment business can just do it to the extreme because of access and money. So someone with an addiction and additive personality and plus have access to money is a recipe for disaster.

I remember someone in Yonkers was trying to get me to bring X to him to buy his drugs; what made that so bad he wasn't the only one. I was approached on several occasions by someone who wanted me to give X the latest this or that. It took me a minute to figure it out, but when I did I learned more about human nature. It was broken down to me from a business perspective. They said think about it if I can get one customer like DMX, the individual said that he could have some money for his daughter's education or possibly save some money for the future for a down payment on a home. So from a business perspective, he wanted X as one of his drug clients.

Therefore, I started to think about who is making the money off selling drugs to entertainers, models, and athletes. It was told to me that was a drug dealer's paradise just to have a short run in some of those circles. Think about it Flava Flav spent over $5.7 million on drugs in 6 years. That's approximately $2,600 a day.

How do you think his life changed by having Flava as a client?

On April 4, 2011 Rapper Lil Webbie in Marshal County Tennessee was arrested on drug charges. According to the reports, the Rapper rented a 2010 Nissan Altima and was pulled over. Cops found 2 ounces of marijuana and $13,240 in cash. According to reports Lil Webbie was sitting on the passenger seat and was trying to throw all of the marijuana out of the window. Webbie and the other passengers of the car were held overnight on a $21,000 bond. A year earlier, his label mate and songwriter friend Lil Boosie caught a charge of first degree murder and drug charges.

I look around and in every social circle I see the same social ills manifest and just take different forms. The average person cannot imagine going to a party at a mansion, luxury suite or an exotic estate to a party that they could never fathom. Some of the prettiest women the eyes can view having orgies in every room that you go into. The finest of food and drink and special tables for all the drugs you can think of, all for your pleasure.

You can consume all that you heart desires and even take some home with you it will not even put a dent in their stash. You are guaranteed to see a few very powerful people from different parts of the world there. Everyone says "What happens in Vegas stays in Vegas!" Yet, Vegas has nothing on these people! In my search for answers about drug addiction, substance abuse or some say the medication of the inner pain. I realized it was intricate and it went into the science of psychology/psychiatry the issues were far serious. The answers must come from mental institutions and professionals.

When I started doing my research on drugs and mental health, I quickly realized that some people I came across in my life had some mental health issues but back in the hood we would just say that nigga crazy. Now I realize, "The nigga was really crazy for real!" Then I thought about the dog.

On December 20, 2010 he was sent to the flamenco mental health unit. It is a facility located inside of the Alabama Prison Complex. The judge who sentenced X noted he may suffer from some sort of mental affliction or may suffer from bi-polar disorder. I was saying to myself, I knew something was wrong with him, but I could never put my finger on it!

I always knew dog was crazy and as for the bi-polar disorder, I'm still learning what the symptoms and side effects are. But I'm wondering is that why DMX was one way in the day time and different at night.

Then a couple weeks later Gucci Mane is committed to a mental health institution. He had pled a special plea of mental incompetency. His position was that he was unable to intelligently participate in the probation revocation hearing. From that day on, I truly realized that the culture I love is having some real serious problems. These problems are affecting the artist, practitioners of the culture and many others. As stories unfold daily I found myself talking to people who had the slightest concern about the issue, and the others that had something's to say needed to be diagnosed as well. So, I sought out a professional to shed a little light on the subject of drugs and addition to give me some clarity.

Drug Dependence, Substance Abuse and Addiction

By: Larmia Robbins-Brinson, Ph.D.
Clinical Psychologist

The Diagnostic and Statistical Manual of Mental Disorders-Text Revision (DSM-IV-TR) is published by the American Psychiatric Association and is the most widely used tool to diagnose mental illness. Information for this chapter comes from the DSM-IV-TR 2009 edition.

To understand addiction, we need to understand the current terminology. Addiction is a term used by the general population to mean problematic use of a substance; however in the mental health arena the terms substance dependence and substance abuse are used. We cannot diagnosis a person as “addicted.”

Substance Dependence vs. Substance Abuse

Let’s shed some light on the two diagnosable categories. The first diagnosis is **substance dependence**. Dependence means a person compulsively continues to use a substance despite significant problems. There must also be repeated patterns of substance use that causes tolerance to the substance. Tolerance means there is a need for greatly increased amounts of the substance to achieve intoxication or there is a diminished effect even when using the same amounts of the substance. Actual tolerance varies between substances and between individuals, but it must be present for dependence to be diagnosed. It is interesting

to note that cannabis users are not usually aware of increased tolerance; however laboratory findings support that tolerance occurs. Substance dependence also has to have some type of withdrawal symptoms. Withdrawal typically has to do with unpleasant physical changes that can spur the person back to substance used to reduce the discomfort; for example, taking a drink of alcohol in the morning to get rid of a hangover headache or to calm the shakes. Withdrawal also leads to craving the substance in many cases. Lastly, substance dependence means the person has expressed a desire to abstain from using the substance and failed.

Substance Abuse is similar to dependence and shares some common characteristics. Abuse consists of a pattern of substance use that significantly impairs ability to fulfill major role obligations such as work and family life. Abuse also means there is repeated use of the substance even when there is a physical hazard such as driving while intoxicated or using dangerous equipment.

With this group there are also repeated legal problems resulting from substance use such as DUI or arrests for disorderly conduct. In addition, abuse is diagnosed when there is continued substance use in spite of problems with relationships. With abuse, there are no symptoms of withdrawal or tolerance.

In an effort to balance out the substance effects it is important to note that dependency upon life-sustaining drugs such as insulin is not diagnosed unless there is a pattern of misuse. It is also possible for someone to be dependent upon pain medications due to illness or injury without abusing the drug. The main concern with substance dependence and abuse is how the person uses the substance in their lives and whether or not there are negative consequences associated with use. Once a pattern of abuse leads to dependence, the cycle is difficult to break. This is why we see entertainers in the revolving doors of rehabilitation centers. Unfortunately, the research on substance dependence is clear that without appropriate interventions, the dependence will lead to premature death.

So what does all this mean?

Substance dependence is a vicious cycle that ensnares the lives of many. Substance abuse and dependence knows no racial boundaries and impacts every socioeconomic level. The various drugs used do have some correlation to race and locality, but the overall problem hits everyone. As with most social problems we don't act to fix it unless it impacts us personally. Typically, we tolerate loved ones who show signs of periodic substance abuse just to keep peace. So people avoid the drunken uncle at the family party unless there is a pressing reason to address the situation. Americans are fiercely independent minded and we allow others to spiral down the path of substance abuse and substance dependence because we don't want to invade their privacy. There are also those who secretly abuse substances such as painkillers or sleep aids and we turn a blind eye. Unless there is a medical crisis that brings the behavior to light, people avoid asking questions of loved ones. In addition, some people believe substance abuse or dependence is a moral failure and should be treated with disdain and left for the person to handle with God.

All-in-all, substance abuse and dependence impacts all of us on some level or another. A co-worker that does not show up, a family member that ruins a special occasion or an impaired driver that could take our lives are a few examples.

Hip-Hop and Marijuana

Although hip hop music began with an image of young people expressing themselves lyrically instead of fighting in the streets, today's entertainers are laden with lavish images of drug use, promiscuous behaviors and excessive consumerism. Unfortunately, there are too many situations where life is imitating art and entertainers find themselves in rehab. It's fair to say, every type of mainstream entertainers have their share of substance dependent individuals. So, it's not only hip-hop but other genres that showcase a life-style of drug abuse. It's also fair to say the image of reggae artists includes marijuana use in addition to the rap artists.

The challenge is for the fans of the artists to enjoy the music without following in the footsteps of substance abuse. Rarely are the dangers of such life styles addressed. Aside from potential legal issues, marijuana use can negatively impact mental health. For example, recent research suggests that marijuana use might speed up the onset of psychosis. An online article in the Health Day Reporter by Amanda Garder published February 2011, stated, "Smoking marijuana might trigger an earlier onset of psychosis…Among people who developed a psychotic illness, those who had smoked pot developed the illness almost three years earlier than those who hadn't." The researchers also found that marijuana may actually cause psychosis in some patients. The complete study is in the June 2011 issue of the Archives of General Psychiatry.

Because of the emulation of rap artist by teens and children, images encouraging marijuana use are especially harmful. "Heavy cannabis use starting at a young age carries a very much greater risk than modest use as an adult," stated study author Dr. Matthew Large, a senior staff psychiatrist at Prince of Wales Hospital in Sydney in the online article by Garder.

In conclusion, there is a difference between substance dependence and substance abuse and addicted is a term from pop culture. There is hope for individuals struggling with drug abuse who choose to enter treatment. However, if there is no intervention and the individual is not willing to seek treatment, then that person is guaranteed an early death.

For more information visit The U.S. National Institute on Drug Abuse website.

WE ARE FAMILY

This chapter will examine the different dynamics of doing business with family in the entertainment industry. Many agree that there are many pros and cons but most people I know in the industry have all outsiders handling their personal financial affairs. I can see the logic in that choice especially if the family member is not knowledgeable in that particular subject matter. Then it would be a good business practice to deal with a seasoned professional to get the job done. Such as accounting and subjects that need attention of a lawyer.

Well how about a family member playing the role of a manager to the artist? Or just on the scene in some capacity looking out for the best interest of their family member?

Some say having family around your business is the worst thing you can have or at least that's the general consensus amongst some in the black community. No matter where I am in the US and the subject of business and family comes up, someone will always refer me to Biggie's first album the song entitled "10 crack commandments."

Crack Commandment #7 this rule is underrated: "***Keep your family and your business completely separated. Money and blood don't mix like two dicks and no bitch; find you in serious shit*** (The Notorious BIG)."

So with that being said, I began to realize that when it comes to the business part of the music it destroys long term relationships and families. In some cases its headlines news all over the world and almost all ends up in court with hefty lawsuits.

I remember someone saying that the game is dirty and they are going to get robbed from someone weather it's an accountant embezzling a few thousands here and there or a manager with access to some of the finances. So the position was why can't a family member get a piece of the pie. If that's the way the game is being played anyway. Yet, there are many examples of family doing business together in the entertainment industry and having some success. Most of the people I talk to argued the fact that African Americans haven't developed to that point as of yet. Their positions for their arrangement were envy, greed, lack of education and unity. When I was told that I took what they said and examined my community and other communities alike throughout New York.

I first looked at the Mexicans and remembered when I was young how they were just settling into town. I would always see groups of them gathering early in the morning on different corners in Yonkers with their tools trying to get some work and you would see people pull up and a few of them got into their trucks and vans and everyone would make some money. In return the person that hired them can also be productive in accomplishing their task at hand.

Now, in 2011 I still see a large Mexican community, but now they own the construction companies. I use Main Street for example they started off with one business, now they own almost every business on the block.

In Manhattan you have china town and little Italy in Williamsburg, Brooklyn you have a strong Jewish community. In the Bronx you have Jerome Ave/Gunhill Rd., and that's a strong Jamaican and West Indian community. You also have a huge Spanish population in Harlem to name a few. I looked at those communities and cultures with the intentions of examining the elements that breeds their success and unity and strength. I asked questions trying find out the core of their success.

Then, I ask a question to myself again why can't the African American unify in Hip Hop because we all agree that the culture changed many of our lives and our family's lives?

I wasn't just going to accept the saying money and blood don't mix. I started seeing that saying as another saying that black folks just pick up and pass along through the generations. If you examine the saying you can see that it's not an absolute truth. All other cultures have family businesses and they keep the money in their families and in their communities. Another example of family and blood is the Italian mafia. While examining the foundations of other cultures in NY I realize that all of them have a strong economic base. With that being said, I don't buy the statement money and blood doesn't mix. Maybe the saying just applies to the African Americans because when I think about it they are the only ones that I hear say that. A lot of sayings that grandma says at the dinner table is wisdom. But a lot of these sayings that people are quoting are just fables and myths that cause psychological damage in the black community.

Another one that doesn't make sense to me is the saying "Don't fight fire with Fire" that saying can be examined from different perspectives. I know if one studies the different way the firemen put out fire. It is recorded on many occasions that sometimes firemen start a fire to help contain or put out the bigger fire so that's another myth. There are so many more, but back to the subject at hand. I had a conversation with a businessman and friend who I would just call Patel who built his fortune from owning hotels and gas stations. I'm into the hip hop business and I come from a town rich in culture. My question to him was what would you have done from a business man point of view if you had some of this music money? Oh that's easy he replied, I would have done the same thing I did with my other businesses except I would have had a bigger budget.

Example: All of my inner circle would have been family members, my lawyers, and accountants. If they weren't in a position of control, they would have been getting groomed for those positions. To build my hotel empire, I sent family members to college and they came back to run businesses. If I was into hip hop I would have sacrificed the platinum chains, some luxury cars, and put a few family members in school immediately. With a five year business plan, I would have increased my profits tremendously. Besides, law, medicine, and business, I would have someone to specialize in real estate and my sister in law would have been finding ways to invest the profits in effort to create what we call wealth.

Now let me ask you a question, you come from a town that has been successful in music for over 20 years. With all the influence and money made over the years and all of the different groups that came from your town, I ask you, what have you all done collectively (for example Motown, etc.)? Do any of them work together? Do y'all have a strong-hold in the industry?

As for real estate I would have also purchased a big estate but the difference is that I would have had several families living in the house instead of just my immediate family. With the other families in the house, we would have done what is tradition in my culture and that is we would have all saved our money and cut our expenses. In a couple of years, we would all have big estates. It's easier for us because we work together so the results are greater and more rewarding.

After speaking to Patel, my mentality about this hip hop money changed. I began looking for ways to maximize my profits. I knew it was going to take team work and patience, which I had but some people around me have little of both. But, I know teamwork is real work. So I kept my team around me and kept working our plan.

As I reflected on the saying "Money and Blood don't mix" then I examined the saying "Blood is thicker than water," seems to only apply to and is real to some people except when doing business. These myths or sayings can get confusing, which is why I took the time to check out some entertainers who have had family members involved in their business affairs.

I examined the super star Beyoncé and discovered her wonderful relationship with her father and manager Matthew Knowles. It is recorded that Matthew Knowles and his wife were entrepreneurs and were successful in business. Through knowledge and hard work along with application provided a good example for Beyoncé and groomed her for success and super stardom.

The superstar Usher Raymond is managed by his mother Jonetta Patton and Usher is rated by the RIAA as one of the best-selling artists in American history. To this date he has sold over 65 million records worldwide. He is a recipient of many prestigious awards such as

Grammy American Music Award, and The Billboard Music Awards. I'm not concerned about their personal business, but their collective body of work as a team speaks for itself.

Then, the world of hip hop saw the Dean Family build Ruff Ryder's from the Ground up, 2 brothers and sister working together to achieve a common goal. I was there I saw it with my own eyes. I studied and tried to emulate those that are successful. I know today as well as in the past that family can work together if you do a little research you will find some more positive examples of teamwork.

All my life, I considered people that I had love for as family. They didn't necessarily have to be blood related. If you are connected with each other, ate, fought, snored, and got paid together then you are a part of what I consider as family.

When I was younger, I just thought everyone cared about each other with all that What's up lingo, all the hugs, and hi fives. I see now that all of that is just some bullshit. Most of it looks and sounds good but it voids substance. As I flashback to the 90's when the dog was younger, he spent his youth with me and his uncle Collie J. Those were some of the best times of my life. We didn't have any money but we had a lot of dreams and plans on what we were going to do. Then people started hearing dog and it brought them to town from far and near. The dog popped his chain and started running wild. To this day I still believe that dog must have gotten infected or bit by a stray dog. Maybe he even caught rabies. His attitude changed I saw signs of anxiety and aggressiveness. Then I saw signs of apprehension, solitude and out of the blue he was snapping on his care takers. I also noticed that he became furious and restless. All the above signs of a dog that has been exposed to rabies and I'm inclined to think that's why my man DMX flipped on me because the disease had an adverse effect on his brain. I guess time and life will vaccinate him and eventually the virus can get out of his system.

Collie J:

What is Collie J's relationship to DMX? He is his uncle by his eldest brother. They grew up together from about 7-8 years of age until their early 20's. Collie lived on Lamartine and he used to come over on the weekends.

It was all love you know we shared the same food, slept in the same bed. We were the same age, which is why we were together all of the time.

In the beginning of his music career I was the first dude in his camp. Don't forget X used to beat box for this other kid in the past. Something happened in the family and X went away to a group home. One day he wrote me and told me that he wasn't beat boxing anymore that he was becoming an MC, and he wrote me a rhyme. When he came home he said something to me that was very impressive. At that time LL was my man, and he sounded like him he had a clear voice, catchy lyrics I told him he has some skills, and he was around 16-17 years old. His abilities were much higher than the average. He said that he was still keeping the name DMX, but he was going to MC instead, no more beat boxing, and it was on from there.

Superior didn't step onto the scene until X and Tashera moved to Mulford. Shortly after that X and Superior started doing the now classic mixed tapes. Before Superior stepped onto the scene it was just him and myself running around Yonkers. I was hitting my chest making the beat and he rhymed. Then, he went to mixed tapes and that era came in with Ron-G, Kid-Capri in the late '80's early '90's. They were up in Yonkers putting work in.

Since stardom our relationship is nowhere as close as we used to be. The lights, cameras, and action have changed things. Part of that was the fact that in the early 90's I was in the streets hustling and at that time you can make an easy $1,000 a day posted up on the corner. I was real heavy into the drug game and he's running around Yonkers with the dog, doing occasional robberies and getting high. I wasn't really messing with him like that because I was doing the drug dealer thing making money, and he was doing the addict thing fucking up money. It just didn't mix because it was bad business.

He was my family and when he had problems in the street he would let me know and we would get at it however. Family is still family, so when they jumped him it was on. He would tell me what's up, and I was like fuck it whatever, let's go get 'em; but after that I went back to making money and he went back to fucking up money. When he was doing music and he wanted me there I was with him at all of the School 12 joints. I was the only person there from Yonkers when he did his first show at the Palladium besides this dude Jack that he was signed to. I trooped it out for my nephew I took a Yonkers union cab down to Manhattan. I was there at the palace and when he did the show at the Castle with Kid Capri and Big Daddy Kane I held him down. I was that dude that was always there in the early stages.

He was talented and I believed in him. I had to always hear him say how nice he was as were going around battling dudes ripping them apart all day on the mic. I was the uncle the hype man. Eventually it led us to Bill Blass and the DMX battle. To keep it 100 (real) my nephew is a very talented individual, but somewhere down the line he allowed the fame and the game to throw him off. However, his overall talent as a mc is pretty much untouchable by most.

He would take rhymes and say them backwards or he would spell a rhyme out he was really hungry and dominant like Mike Tyson. When he came out no one could touch him. It was a shock to me because I have never been around anyone that hungry before, with that much passion for anything. He was an overall talent and should be top dog today, but he put the wrong people and elements in his life.

Why did you do the interview on VH1?

I was surprised to get a call from him to be honest because we haven't spoken in a long, long time. Considering our relationship and history we should be much closer "Blood in Blood out." I had to do it I couldn't shit on him because at the end of the day we are still family. We may have a love/hate relationship, but he's my nephew, which is why I did the show and gave him some love. Now, the other side of the story is what I need to say to him face to face there were no regrets.

The only thing that I can't get over is what he did to Superior. My nephew says "He keeps it real," my manz and them and stop being greedy; but he did Superior Greazy. That really fucked me up because Superior was his backbone and in my opinion if it wasn't for Superior his foundation wouldn't have been as strong. He was nice on his own, but Superior was the center or the head of the operation. He put all of the music out in the streets; he did the street promotions without all of that his buzz wouldn't have been as heavy.

TASHERA & XAVIER

I don't know who was on that bullshit and started influencing him, but they pushed him away from his original team of people that had his back. At one point it was just X, Superior, Tashera, and myself, but when the money came in a lot of people were pushed to the side and others moved in. Just look at who is successful and who benefited the most, and who has the most money. The people that did music for X and care about him were jerked the most or received nothing. On principle I don't respect what he did to Superior. I have been rolling tight through thick and thin with my boy Al for 30 years, and that's how you're supposed to be with your people. I blame the entire business itself and all of those entities. He was a dude that didn't have a lot of money and had a rep for living in the streets. When that money came it took him somewhere different and he never came back.

By him separating himself from his core foundation that is a primary reason he's going through his situations today. Half of the things he's done in the streets over the years he would never have done when we were on the scene; such as driving without a license, and impersonating an officer. All he has around him lately are yes men. They don't have any say so. I know that I am not a yes man. I cracked dudes heads to the white meat for him in the streets of Warburton. They are there for one thing and one thing only and that's the money and when they're finished with him it's on to the next one. I'm not saying his label and management is 100% to blame because he is his own man; but they just pushed him somewhere different. Looking back at it now I realize that he probably didn't know how to take control of his situation.

There are a lot of things that I would like to say to my nephew from my heart right now. He could have really cornered the industry at that time, because it was all happening when Def Jam was the biggest label in the country and DMX was the headliner. The wrong forces came in and dictated how he was supposed to run this thing, now look at his situation he has a tarnished legacy. Why is DMX not on the list of the top 10 rappers of all time? Check out his body of work and you draw your own conclusions. In a 3 year span my nephew sold 20 million records. They used things that happened in his personal life to cripple his music accomplishments. The **"Yes Man"** destroyed his career and took it somewhere else.

In conclusion, I would like to say know yourself and remember where you came from, because you might have to go back there. Remember where you came from and who helped you to get there, and that will bring you back to the top. Why is he not on the cover of Forbes?

However, I do see him on the internet news getting locked up or coming out of jail. It's really a sad story for someone with that much talent.

How are you giving back to the kids?

I have been working for the last 10 years at the Nepperhan Community Center working with the youth. In the late '90's I was doing a lot of negative things and was going back and forth to the penitentiary doing state bids. On my last bid I was in the max and I saw what was really going on. It is a major business and black men are the major products. Every Tuesday a bus would come with two or three hundred people mostly black. They would be shipped off to another facility and they work for minimum wage. I was like I couldn't be a part of this business because all that was in it for me and the rest of those involved was suffering and pain. That's when I decided that when I got home I was going to make a change for the youth. In the mountains all I saw were 18 and 19 year olds coming through camp getting 15-20 years as though it was nothing. They were smiling and playing as though it was a joke, I told them this is your life. So, I came home in 2000 with the mind state to help the youth.

Now, I wanted to be a role model for the youth, because I caught my case on Warburton for "Intent to sell," I did 3-6 yrs. That is why I'm flipping it now. The people who saw me selling drugs in the streets all day, now see me working with the kids all day. I want people to say if he could do it so can I. I would give the children assistance on how to stay out of the game, and I have been doing it for the last 10 years. I see the works of my good labor!

We have a program called action youth, which focuses on kids in the school system. They are children who are kicked out of the regular school system and come to our program for about four months, and then go back to the regular school system. In my travels I see about 15-20 kids that were kicked out of school for fighting, weapons, etc. now they have jobs, apartments and are seeing their way they are on the right path. These children have completed a total transformation.

One of the kids was thought to be one of the baddest kids in Yonkers because of his activities in school and the streets; however, now he has a child, a job, a car, and a diploma. I used to talk to him a lot and spend quality time with him while he was in the program. When he sees me he shows me love and acknowledges what role I played in helping to save his life.

If you're talking about numbers, on the low end if I am able to help at least one kid a year I would be successful in my mission.

DMX as a PASTOR?

(Tina) -Well let me answer this first since I'm the only female here. First, and foremost, I will say for the record, DMX has one of the best deliveries I have ever heard. I love his voice and he speaks from his soul. When I hear him, sometimes I have to fold my arms because I get goose bumps.

I also enjoy when he prays in the form of a poem/rhyme. They are deep and heartfelt. Those are his prayers coming from his soul to his creator, agreeable or disagreeable, but because some make good music, that doesn't mean I will follow them when it comes to things of the spirit. (I am not a groupie when it comes to my soul!)

(Greg)-Let me interject and say, I think he will bring a lot of people to church, especially those that haven't been there in a long time. Maybe he's called to do the work of God.

(Chris) -I don't know y'all. The soul is very serious. My question is; if DMX becomes a preacher, will he be teaching the slave Christianity? That's all I want to know! I need more than prayers and sermons to impress me, because most of that stuff is orchestrated. You know how the organ, and the preacher work together to stimulate certain emotions. Y'all know how they do? Or do y'all?

I send the Brother my blessings. I would like to tell him not to play with souls, putting on a grand production. I hope you keep the fire in you. Some will debate me on this, but the church makes black men soft, and passive. I often think about turn the other cheek. Now, you kept it real in your music please don't turn into a sucker.

Word, X is from the streets of YO. I know he ran across knowledge of self in some form. They said DMX means Divine Master of the unknown, that's old 5% jargon. I'm just going to sit back and see what type of warrior he really is, or is he going to be a monkey?

(Tina)- Is he studying some of the ancient languages? At least if he's going to teach from the bible he should be studying some Hebrew, because comparing the English, Latin, and Greek to Hebrew, you will see a lot was left out in the translation. That will be a question I would like to ask him. To most that don't matter, but to me language is important, it is the very foundation. If he doesn't have Hebrew translations or an understanding of it, I'm definitely not going to take him too serious when it comes to having an in-depth overstanding of the Bible scripture.

So the first question I would ask DMX is how many languages he speaks? And please, I hope he doesn't give me that lame excuse of it doesn't matter, because simple comparisons of some words in the bible all prove otherwise.

Another question I would like to ask Mase, Hammer or any other rapper turned minister is, are they familiar with the Nicene Council?

By their answer it will reveal a lot to me about their knowledge level of Christianity. My final question would be what Jesus does he follow? Simon Bar Jesus of the book of Acts 13 or Y'ashua Ha Mashiak (Hebrew) (Jesus the Messiah)? The reason I would ask that question is because most people get them confused, or don't know that more than one Jesus exists in the bible. The three Jesus' are Jesus the Messiah, Simon Bar Jesus (Acts 13), Jesus Justus son of Mark Anthony and Cleopatra and Google the tomb of Jesus found in Kashmir, India.

Which Jesus do you follow?

Simon Bar Jesus was a sorcerer who performed magic and bewitched people. His mother was named Mary also and is said to have hung out with Paul. This Simon Bar Jesus had a huge following also because the magic he was performing his followers called it miracles. Don't forget his name was Simon Bar Jesus which is a Hebrew word for son (**check it out**).

(Greg): I heard Mase is growing in the word and is building a good foundation in Christ under the tutelage of Creflo Dollar.

(Tina): I heard that too! My grandmother said it looks as though the spirit was working with him and he was bringing younger people back into the body of Christ. She was pleased but she was very disappointed when he released another album with 50 Cent. I saw tears come from her eyes. She was more concerned with the mixed messages he was sending. My grandmother was quoting lyrics from Mase and said to me, "The church ain't big enough to buy what I'm buying! And Diddy ain't give enough to fly what I'm flying." She went on to say he's back on the gangster rap materialism mentality.

(Dave): What's wrong with that?

(Chris): Come on y'all he's a pastor he or they will say this is my art or craft, and it has nothing to do with my faith or religion. It's about business and money. So out of one side of your mouth you talk about your guns, dope and hoes. Then, on Sunday you're holy. I'm confused it seems like you can do anything in this modern day Christianity. What does it mean when it is said that you can't serve two masters? Personally, I think that most of them are running game. They want influence, money, attention, but besides music and entertainment the church is a way to get all of the above. People are so star struck and spellbound they are willingly surrendering their souls.

(Tina): What gave me inspiration during some hard times was DMX's song Lord Give Me a Sign. It touched me deep down inside. I would be driving to that song and I love when he says in the name of Jesus and he quotes "No weapon formed against me shall prosper," that gives me motivation. Then on the hook he sings: ***"Lord give me a sign": "Let me know what's on your mind. Let me know what I'm going to find it's all in time. Show me how to teach the mind, show me how to reach the blind Lord give me a sign. Show me what I gots to do to bring me closer to you 'cause I'm going to go through whatever you want me to. Show me what I got to do."*** I love that song and the lyrics are hard.

(Dave): I like when he says ***"trapped in your own mind waiting on the Lord, I'm hunting like the word that cuts like a sword***." I agree that song is hot. That inspires me like "Jesus walks" by Kanye West. X has a lot of good prayers in his collection that I enjoy. I will start with the song "Ready to meet him" from the album "Flesh of my flesh blood of my blood.

I like the lyrics when he says: ***"Thank you Lord for my birth and everything that follows, I thank you Lord***

for today and I will pray for tomorrow. I thank you Lord for the love of my life and a friend. I made a promise I'm loving my wife to the end. " I like to kick back with a glass of wine and vibe on that.

(Greg): Have you ever heard the song "A minute for your son" off the great depression album, that song is hot too. He's also paying homage to the heavenly father. The hook is really catchy, and it goes like this- ***"Lord you got me like, your love got me like"*** (repeat). It has a nice rhythm to it, and X sounds like he's happy on that song.

I remember we were having family dinner one Sunday and everyone was choosing an inspirational song, mom dukes was on her Warren Sapp vibe so she played it like five times in a row. My uncle put "We fall down" in heavy rotation. When it was my turn I told them I was going to play some DMX, my uncle grabbed the bible and started praying from the book of psalms.

Everyone in the house went crazy; you should have seen what I went through trying to convince them that it was positive and inspirational. After 10-15 minutes they let me play the song. When the song first came on their faces were tight then the beat drop and 20 seconds into the song I saw grandma tapping her feet. I was like yeah and I started dancing with grandma, then it was on. We were rocking then everyone else loosened up.

When the hook came on the second time the entire house was singing – ***"Lord you got me like, Love you got me like***…"we had a good time. Next it opened them up to other things I had to offer. Therefore, because I had the floor I hit 'em with the prayer from "It's dark and hell is hot" and it goes like this –

"***I come to you hungry and tired you give me food and let me sleep. I came to you weak; you give me strength now that's deep.***

You call me a sheep;

you lead me to green pastures only asking that I keep the focus in between the chapters.

You give me the word and only ask that I interpret then, give me the eyes that I may recognize the serpent. We know I ain't perfect, but you like want me to lie until I die. Lord why is it that I go through so much pain all I saw was black all I felt was rain."

When X got to that part when I looked around and everyone was in awe, a few people had their hands up, and some were saying amen. That's when I knew that X touched them. At that moment it left a powerful impression on my family especially when Uncle Calvin started crying. We played that prayer about five times in a row.

Yes, his prayers are awesome, but that doesn't necessarily mean that he can make the transition to become a preacher or does it?

My question to him would be what are you going to be teaching? That would be my primary concern if he is going to be teaching. With all of the albums that I have purchased I want to hear a warrior doctrine. I want to hear a resurrection doctrine. He talks about and acknowledges the power of the lord. I want to see what he is really teaching because if he's pushing the slave teachings of the spook god I would rather just enjoy him rapping and recite his inspiration prayers.

(Greg) Why are you so hard?

(Chris) It's a big responsibility to stand in a position of power like that with that amount of attention and already being under so much scrutiny. Think about it for a moment politicians and preachers are looked at under a super microscope. I just don't want to see him take a fall like that because I love him as an artist and I can stick with him through his ups and downs as an artist. There are plenty of artists that we can think of that had problems with drugs and the law; we sit and watch television and talk around the water cooler and say things like did you see such and such don't they look bad, or look they're in trouble again. I or someone would say I hope they get their act together because I love their music or their acting abilities. We would listen to the new reports, however in the back of our mind and deep in our heart we would really be rooting for them and we would pray for their eventual victory. I'm always rooting for the underdog. But, on the other side of it, I'm not even a Christian, so I will probably get more from his fine collections of albums than from him preaching an English Bible.

(Greg) But, that's when your faith comes in!

(Chris) Faith is important, but how about the facts, the logic, the common sense, the confirmation of everything that is going on in the era that we are in now. I need more than just blind faith.

(Greg) That's cool, I never looked or thought about that in that perspective.

(Tina) You're right in that regards because in this information age it is making it hard to lie to people. There is too much knowledge available the world has the ability to become more informed. People are not being just lead blindly any more.

My father was a Public Enemy fan; and he made me listen to it when I was growing up. Now, when I look back on it that was a blessing because Public Enemy at the time was bringing awareness and consciousness through music and it was waking people up to a degree. I say all of that to say lately a friend of mine put me up on Professor Griff, and he is teaching, lecturing, and writing books and saying controversial things.

(Greg) What is he talking about?

(Tina) He is talking about how hip-hop is changing, the industry, and what's going on behind the scene. What he said that caught my attention is the frequency of hip-hop is being changed so I had to investigate that. It just made me think about music, harmonies, vibrations, and tones. I studied some natural music, synthetic music, and how it affects us as a people.

You know how music can make you feel good or make you want to hurt something. Just through a little research on the sounds of music, I realize how certain tones and melodies can affect you and make you respond in certain ways. I confirmed that observation watching a church sermon, and I noticed how the organ was used to bring intensity to the sermon when the pastor is at his highest point, and can hit another note to make you cry. I was like wow. So, now I realize when I listened to hip-hop music over the past couple of years I noticed a lot of high pitched frequencies, synthetic drums, low base tones, and vibrations. It just makes me think that frequency is going out into the universe laced with bad grammar. Just do a simple study and you will notice the music has changed every 10 years or so.

Let's start at 1945 there was Duke Ellington, Louise Armstrong, and Billy Holliday notice their sound, their melody and tone. Next, go to 1955 Stevie Wonder, Sam Cooke, James Brown, Patti Labelle, and Smoky Robinson and the miracles notice that era and sound. Then, go to 1965 with Miles Davis, Brass Constitution, Donna Summer, The Temptations, Earth Wind and Fire, The Jackson 5, and Aretha Franklin just to name a few. A lot of the really great music from those groups carried over into the 1970's, and that era also had some wonderful music. Personally, I think after that era that type of music just started to slip away. The tone changed, the language changed, the mind state changed. Real instruments were replaced with electronic machines, now look what we have…think about it. (Refer to Are there Black Devils by: Dr. York).

(Chris) Well, why we are on that subject there are a lot of young people talking about hip-hop and satanic worship. There is a lot of talk about artists throwing up satanic signs of 666 and Bahomet signs. Do y'all think that's just a coincidence? I mean these are the same signs the heavy metal satanic worshippers and people of the occult utilize. Is there any substance to that?

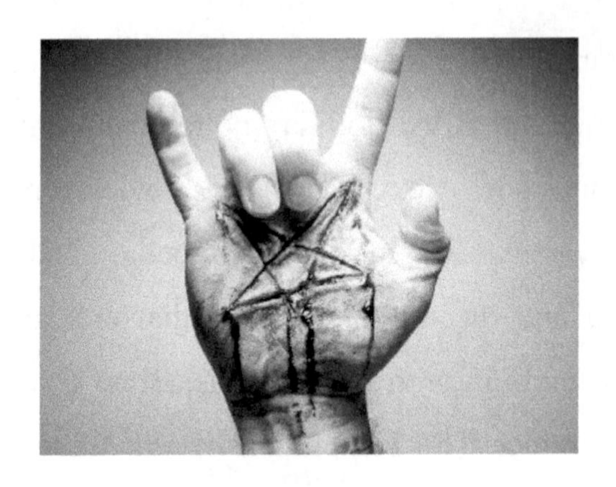

Personally, I am not concerned with the pyramid sign because I studied the culture of ancient Egypt and I know all science and civilization in the world came out of Egypt. Moreover, all was taught from the Egyptian mystery schools, and I was reminded that Satanists utilize ancient Egyptian symbols in their orders and rituals. Nonetheless a pyramid doesn't indicate satanic worship to me saying a pyramid is satanic can be deception.

However, people use symbols take them as their own and add their own twist to them; but, regardless of what anyone says to me I know historically a satanic worshipper only uses certain symbols. Therefore, if a rapper is throwing up the same signs as a satanic worshipper I have to raise my eyebrows, and not care who he or she is!

You know how the hood is they will take something and add their own twist to it and call it something else. Or, they will remix it like some did with the word "nigga." So, regardless of how it's flipped and bounced around as time goes by it still means the same thing. I think that if you're throwing up the same sign as the Beetles who were known to dabble in Satanism to me you are suspect!

At times when I look at the music business I think some artists have sold their souls to the devil. Sometimes I think the world is so star struck that they can't see things for what they are even when they are presented with facts. To most it doesn't matter because as soon as the music comes on they will be on the dance floor shaking their ass again. I have taken on the attitude that whatever they do off stage that's on them; it's their life and soul.

(Tina) Are you saying to me that it wouldn't bother you that maybe some of your favorite artists can be devil worshippers?

(Chris) I really can't answer that question right now, but I know Sammy Davis Jr. had many fans, and dealt with Anton Lavey (founder of the Satanic Church) and he had a big following.

Sometimes I think some of these entertainers are naïve of what's going on, or maybe they have reached a point where it's all about money and some don't care anymore. Lyrically I love Kanye West I would put him up there with the best, and I love his classic "Jesus Walks." However, years later I hear him freestyle and he's talking about selling his soul. I was shocked and was like what the hell is he talking about? Then I thought about it maybe he was just being lyrically creative because rappers paint a lot of pictures with their words. They tell stories and develop characters, etc. but I thought these guys paid attention to words due to that being their way of making their money. They know the power of words they're wordsmiths and craftsmen.

(Greg) What did he say?

Kanye West said "***I sold my soul to the devil; I know it's a crappy deal. At least it came with a few toys like a happy meal.***" That lyric right there is airy.

Then, I heard Eminem's lyric "***I never would have rapped I sold my soul to the devil and I'll never get it back***." Tupac said "***selling my soul for material wishes fast cars, and bitches***." Then one of the most shocking interviews I have ever seen was with singer Bob Dylan who admitted on 60 minutes that ***he sold his soul to the devil to get to where he is***. Last but not least our boy DMX on his first album it's dark and hell it hot, his lyric was "***I sold my soul to the devil and the price was cheap. Yo, it's cold on this level, 'cause it's twice as deep, but you don't hear me…"*** So when I hear and see these things that seem to be satanic do I just take them as coincidence, or do I deal with what presented itself to me? I do know one thing; it's easy to push it off as coincidence because then I do not have to deal with the conclusions of things that are beginning to add up. Well, if DMX sold his soul I pray that he gets it back. I pray that the most high restores his soul.

Think about this for a moment, all of these years there have been rumors floating around that the devil controls the music industry. What would make you think that hip-hop was immune? I had to get over the mental obstacles and deal with the evidence and where it led me.

Where it says I sold my soul that is used metaphorically in which they had to compromise so much of themselves and their core values as an individual, and now they feel empty inside. The devil was inside of the details as far as contracts and obligations, etc. I think you then become locked in and lose control; however, it seems like X don't care about that stuff.

In conversations the question always arises, why is he like that? While so many people dream of some of the things he has accomplished. Another question that arises often is how can a man come from nothing, sell over 28 million records, achieve wealth, and seem not to really give a damn?

I think about that often myself but I'm not a psychologist I don't have those answers. He has seen and experienced something that changed his perspective on things. Some say that hip-hop was a sport to him and he just ran through the game because he knew he always could when given a chance.

There has been a lot of talk and information on the internet saying that major hip-hop stars are affiliated with the illuminati. Some say that when you start making millions you start moving in different circles with more obligations and ties to others. Behind the scenes you have a ceiling that you cannot go beyond with the unseen hand, which leads to the illuminati.

(Greg) Are you serious? You're over the top with everything! So, you're saying that the illuminati are taking over hip-hop now? Do you still smoke weed?

No, I don't smoke any more, but if I did would that eliminate the fact that what I am saying there is substance to back it up. Why don't you think the illuminati wouldn't be interested in hip-hop from the limited information I have on the group. One thing that is clear is that they love power and money. Hip-hop has evolved into a multi-billion dollar operation where music influences the masses. I can see how hip-hop can arouse some interest from that group, plus it is said that the illuminati are Satanists, it is also said that the devil is in the music industry. (Refer to the Illuminati the truth behind the music industry, the YouTube video).

(Tina): Do they control or influence hip-hop?

(Chris) I don't know, but I'm happy that information is coming out to make the public aware of this group. The more information we have the better off the world will be. Most young people's introduction to the illuminati has been in you tube where it is saturated with different entertainers and their supposed connection to the group; however, if one truly wants to become more educated they would have to do extensive research on their own. Some of the clippings I see have some flaws; if you're not educated on some things you wouldn't be able to pick it up, you will be informed and misinformed at the same time. It could possibly be the illuminati putting out misinformation themselves to make the cynical and those in doubt have more doubt.

(Tina) Will y'all just stop it already; I'm not into the doom and gloom the illuminati are only a small percentage of the Earth's population. Yes, they control all of the financial institutions, but we the people can relinquish their power. I'm just tired of hearing about them and their plans to take over the world, enough already; I don't want to hear that, why doesn't anyone put out the knowledge about the good illuminati. The word illuminati come from the word illuminate, which equals light, or the light bearers. There are two forms of light, you have your amber light or red light which came from the hot poisonous fire, and you have your green light. They both have power and interest on this planet. All I'm saying is that we need to focus on the green light from the warring Angel Michael and then the Planet Earth will have peace. It's the negative illuminati that are causing all of the mischief on the planet. However, my grand-ma told me that their time is up, their rule has ended.

But, they are not going to give up without a fight.

(Greg) You have given me a different way to look at it now, things are starting to connect, and make a little more sense to me. I wonder if that is one of the reasons why they are going into space so often and build more space stations. I read an article in the past where they mention a hip-hop entertainer buying some property on the moon and other places in space. When I find the article I will share it with you, but I don't think the majority of the people in the hip-hop industry even take the existence of such a group is taken seriously. Most don't care and most are just trying to get paid. Do you remember when rap artist Nas said "***Nigga's play with play-stations, they're building space stations on Mars plotting civilizations.***"

(Dave) Hip-Hop has a message in each story and it has been that way since the beginning. There were those that had a different doctrine and twist on world views such as African Bambatta, Brand Nubian, Eric B & Rakhim, Public Enemy, X-Clan & KRS-One, and Poor Righteous Teachers to name a few. Those pioneers mentioned taught about black culture and raising the mentality of a people. Their messages were liberating and uplifting and were a part of the foundation and core of hip-hop. The foundation of hip-hop was based on mathematics, with that in mind I wonder how Bishop Hezekiah Walker can be given the title hip-hop minister. Since the beginning of the culture you had other major influences, and the groups named above were not Christians.

With a title like that are they saying that hip-hop is Christian?

(Tina) So, maybe DMX has a calling. Who are any of us to say if he does or doesn't, he's responsible for his own soul. Maybe he will become a good pastor and produce great work as he did in the music industry. Time will only tell!

(Greg) You are absolutely correct; I just pray that he becomes informed and learned because there is a lot of information out there. The information that ya'll presented to me earlier in the conversation lit a fire in me to do some research. I just don't want my favorite rapper to step into that world unprepared, and get the kids into him and his word then slip again.

(Chris) I truly understand because that can have negative side effects on those that choose to become a part of his flock; but he can always flip it and get on his 'preacher pimp' and say he who is without sin cast the first stone.

HIP HOP & THE ILLUMINATI

In the last couple of years there has been a buzz in the teenage and young adult circles about the New World Order (N.W.O) the illuminati and hip hop. The first thing that came to my attention was being surprised about the subject matter being spoken upon; secondly, I noticed that most young adults were conversing about the subject, however their sources were mainly YouTube and DVD's.

There are very few who read any books, or did any thorough research on the subject. I listened to the young lady and wrote down her YouTube sites and took the DVD she offered me. I had to take it anyway because I have a homeboy that's in to that stuff and I will just give it to him if I found no use for it. She said peace and I will see you tomorrow with some more info. then, she walked off. I remember saying to myself this young person is really seeking knowledge.

I started to reflect back about 15-20 years ago when the subject of illuminati would come up. It would be quickly swept under the rug by so called educated people and others that were "in the know." However, they really had no knowledge of it or either they denied the existence of such a thing. So my hat went off to her and her friends.

A couple of hours later I received a phone call from Sarah and she said that she had found a credible source on the subject of the illuminati. She gave me the name Jordan Maxwell and said that his information was solid. Sarah began to cross reference things that Maxwell was elaborating on and explained how things began to connect on another level for her. She then explained to me that the group goes back to ancient Babylon, and their mysticism was called illuminism or to be illuminated. They lived dormant for ages then resurfaced again around the time of the age of enlightenment. My next question was who formed or reactivated the illuminati in the 1700's?

Sarah referred me to a book from author Dr. Malachi Z. York "The Year 2000 and What to Expect;" and told me about Adam Weishaupt who resurrected it on May 1,

1776 in Bavaria, Germany. It is recorded that he had knowledge of witchcraft, practiced Catholicism and was also a Jesuit priest. He was also well educated and a professor of law. Eventually he got the attention of Mayor Amschel Rothschild from the family of German Bankers to finance his plan for the new world order. The bankers had plans to take over Earth's natural resources and wealth. The proposal that Weishaupt gave caught their attention.

The slick manipulating Weishaupt was well learned in the science of espionage, and needed a shield to hide his dirty work and push his agenda. Then, he was initiated into masonry and eventually met a very knowledgeable man and high ranking free mason named Baron Von Knigge. The illuminati then began positioning themselves in positions of political, economic, and legislative power to push the diabolical plan to take over the world. I was also referred to a book called "the protocols of the learned Elders of Zion."

She continued to talk about the influence of the group and around the world then eventually she returned to hip hop. She started talking about the rumors of black entertainers making packs with the devil and sacrificing members of the families for success fortune and fame.

This time she is referencing Professor Griff from public enemy and his series of lectures. I was like cool this gives me a reason to examine Griff body of work and also because my daughter ask me a question about masonry based on a lecture given by Professor Griff. I quickly realized that the buzz of the illuminati is circulating in the music industry, and amongst the younger generation.

The question often arises, do masons worship the devil? Are all masons apart of the illuminati and take blood oaths in the Hip Hop circles?

I was led to Professor Griff who has a series of videos on YouTube entitled "the illuminati take over," Professor Griff speaking on "Masons Part 2," and Professor Griff on "the illuminati." As I viewed the footage, I hear mention of Travistock Institute of Human Relations and also some references of the children being attacked with tones and frequencies. I was like, he is making some sense. Then, he started talking about different entertainers taking an oath and making blood sacrifices to obtain success, and several high profile people were mentioned. Then he went into how Kanye West wanted success so bad that he said, and I quote "signed on, became a mason and took the oath wrote Lucifer son of the morning for Jay Z that was his initiation. Sure enough he lost his moms."

My first question was "What do you mean became a mason and took the oath, what Oath?" Are you familiar with the oath that the masons take? Then he goes on to say that Kanye's initiation…Initiation to what? If one would take the time to listen to the song that Jay Z and Kanye recorded there are no lyrics of subliminal suggestion worshiping Lucifer. As a matter of fact the hook goes as follows "Lucifer son of the morning I'm going to chase you out of the earth."

I listened to it several times trying to find mystical meaning and I came to the conclusion that there were none. Then I was trying to figure out how all of this got tied to Kanye sacrificing his mother? It just didn't connect or make sense.

Then in the same series Professor Griff made reference to a t-shirt that Jay Z had on that read "Signs and Symbols control the earth, not phrases and laws." Then Griff says Jay Z was making you aware that he was a part of the illuminati and had taken an oath.

My next question was how does wearing a t-shirt with Masonic symbols indicate that you are part of the illuminati?

I personally am not aware of Jay Z and Kanye West affiliation with the occult. I'm not defending them; I am just asking questions trying to get some clarity. Then I looked at it from another perspective and said maybe Jay Z is a genius and as a businessman he is just exploiting and capitalizing on the ignorance of people. Then Professor Griff goes on to mention a magician by the name of Aleister Crowley and a quote that he is famous for "Do what thou wilt," and showed a picture Jay Z wearing a shirt with that phrase on it. And the footage showed Crowley as a 33 degree Mason.

Now, I'm asking what the link is between masonry and the illuminati?

ALEISTER CROWLEY

Doing a quick study on the subject I realized that most of the people that write about masons are not masons themselves. So how credible can their facts be? Have you ever come across any information that all freemasons worship the devil and make blood sacrifices? If so, what lodges?

If masonry is a worldwide organization that dates back before 1717, and the grand lodge of England has its origins in the Egyptian Mystery School known by few as the Craft of Amen Re; My question would be, how can the infiltration that took place in 1776 Barvara Germany with Weishaupt, Crowley, and others really contaminate the frame work of the craft that has been protected for thousands of years?

From the history of Public Enemy it is obvious that the group was influenced by the honorable Elijah Muhammad and he was a mason, therefore my question to Griff would be did he take an oath?

Well, where did the rumor that masons worship Lucifer come from?

It has its origins in the late 1800's by a man named Jogand Pages a.k.a Leo Taxil 1854-1907. He created a special campaign to smear masonry though numerous books and articles that the organization was satanic in nature. He admitted that his writings were a big hoax. Crowley was a witch and attracted the teachings of

Albert Pike. Crowley was a member of the O.T.O Ordos Temple Orientis. He fashioned his order after free masonry and German illuminism. With that being said, Crowley couldn't have any adverse effect on the rudiments of Masonic brotherhood. If you do your research you will notice that Crowley was never really accepted in masonic circles (refer to the book "Do Free Masons Worship Lucifer?").

In conclusion Professor Griff should make it clearer when he talks about masonry and their involvement in the illuminati instead of generalizing and being vague in his breakdowns when trying to make a connection between the two. Considering his history with black culture, I'm sure he has been exposed to some literature about masonry and its connection and roots to Africa. I would like to have his take on that. Professor Griff, is he an educator, freedom fighter, or exploiter of black folks?

Author Michael Berkley:

Thank you for asking me what I think about the brother, Professor Griff. He is definitely an influential individual within the African Diaspora community. I give reverence to him for his courage in standing up and speaking out against what he feels are dehumanizing, despiritualizing, and deculturalizing practices against Africans. Likewise, I enjoyed him being an important element in the Hip-Hop group, Public Enemy. I enjoyed the precise military drill team movements that I later found to be similar to the Nation of Islam's military group, Fruit of Islam. This was very mind catching as a youth with this in mind; I do not acknowledge him as a scholar nor effective leader for today's people of the African Diaspora. I see him as an agitator of nation building. Also, I see him as an assistant to those focusing on the intellectual sabotage of Africans.

What do I mean by this?

Simply, things have changed from the revolutionary times of the Black Panther Party, Pan-African, Black Nationalism, so-called Black Muslims, and Civil Rights era of the 40s through the 70s. As we have now entered the informational age, the concept of "Knowledge is power" is a reality. One cannot continue to utilize outdated techniques of making other's aware of the atrocities committed on Africans and expect a change to drastically occur. We have easy access to acquiring information beyond concepts which have become the normative in the African in America community.

One factor in the intellectual sabotage is Professor Griff's rhetoric will lead many towards committing a physical suicide as they stand strong on the frontlines of the battlefield with no overstanding of why they are there. These soldiers are not being encouraged to analytically reason nor establish a logical concept beyond the simplicity of the white man's wrongdoings. Again, many of these people are regurgitating the same information that was relayed by the leaders of the 60s. There is a great need to overstand why, when, where, what, and how the white man systematically conceived and implemented whiteness to build nations not at his own hand, but at the hands of other races. This type of knowledge is needed not only for nation building purposes, but for defensive and offensive purpose since we are in a mental warfare.

Another factor in the intellectual sabotage is the cruel, violent, and brutal attack against Freemasonry. Professor Griff is known for saying Freemasons take bizarre oaths as well as they rule the world. As my co-author and I wrote in our book, "***Do Freemasons Worship Lucifer?***" People have joined the order with the intent of learning the inner workings of the craft. If Freemasons established the US, it would only be of common sense to think the US' whole structure can be found in Freemasonry. Further, by researching the history of Freemasonry, they were the ones who fought against the tyranny of the monarchs and the church. In return the monarch and church utilized its influence to verbally attack Freemasons. Additionally, Freemasons are the cause of the economic feudal system coming to an end.

An argument will arise that black Masons do not have the same knowledge as white Masons. I counter argue that too much credit is given to white Masons. A majority of concepts within Freemasonry was taken from ancient Africa. We also wrote about this in our books ***African Origin found in Religion and Freemasonry*** **as well as** ***Religion, Politics, and Freemasonry: a violent attack against Ancient Africa.*** Just as Greeks received philosophy from ancient Egyptians is the same way European Freemasons received Freemasonry from ancient Africa. Many people fail to realize that there is a subject called Freemasonic Philosophy. This is the study of the lessons within Freemasonry. Likewise, people overlook the connection Freemasonry has to France, the occultists. They focus on England. This is a tragic mistake.

The next factor with the intellectual sabotage is Professor Griff's claim that artists take oaths and sacrifice their family members.

If I am not mistaken Professor Griff was within the music industry? So what oath did he take? Did he break his oath when he was kicked out of Public Enemy?

Questions like these arise when one analytically looks at Professor Griff's presentations. However, his demeanor is strong enough to keep people from asking him questions about his personal involvement. He does not have to answer the difficult questions because he has built a reputation of being a warrior against the powers-to-be.

All in all, Professor Griff is utilizing fear to its fullest. He has perfected the ideology and methodology of Capitalism, although he may not be capitalizing totally from his endeavors. His methodology is similar to Christian leaders (i.e. preachers, ministers, bishops, etc.) who scream at the top of their lungs about Satan and Lucifer. It is all fear tactics. Professor Griff is perpetuating the idea of not learning the enemy's methodology. He would rather develop concepts that make little sense except to the people who follow him closely as well as utilize the same information to justify their way of thinking. We are in an age that information is of abundance. As Dr. Amos Wilson once stated, "(Now-a-days) someone has to will their selves to be stupid." This is a mental/ intellectual war not a physical war.

FULL CIRCLE

They say what goes up must come down and as a child I always heard the saying what goes around comes around. When I was younger and naive to life through lack of experience, successes and failures; trial and errors, I just thought it was just sayings that were just picked up from people throughout generations. I never really paid attention to what I, or whomever was saying. I was just repeating what I had heard.

In the back of my mind remembering when my grandmother used to say things like that while we were at the dinner table. She called it the law of karma. I still didn't understand what she was talking about and I didn't see it in my life as of yet so I didn't know how to apply it to myself.

Through time and age, the principles of the words started to become clearer by revealing things to me that changed my life and on some occasions almost scared me to death.

As I continued to walk in life, one day I ended up down in Harlem trying to find some coats for my daughter and I ran into this young man selling books on what he called actual facts. I told him the only fact that I'm concerned about is that if I don't get the coats for my daughter, I'm going to be in a bad situation. "How you like that? Why don't you put that in your book?" To my surprise he only smiled, and that threw me off because I was looking for a different reaction from him. In the moment that I was stumbling he said cool brown man, no harm intended. "You look like someone who has some business about himself and in my experiences those are the type of people that read these books. Then I looked him up and down noticing that he was clean, neat and well shaved. Then, I eyeballed his wife and couldn't help but notice that big rock on her hand, which made me give him a minute of my time because in my travels most people that push culture or talk that talk is always broke. He was the complete opposite.

Then he said these are scrolls or actual facts it talks about nature and your relationship with nature. What he said that caught my attention is that he mentioned the nature of nature, universal laws, principles, and the law of opposites.

When he said universal laws he flashed me back to the dinner table with my grandma talking about the law of karma. I was saying to myself damn, is this what my grandma meant when she said that I will meet people in my travels that will know the laws? Then, I asked about karma and asked is it real. He went on to explain that there were laws of nature and laws of the universe. He started really simple with cause and effect for every action there is an opposite and equal reaction, stimulus, and response. I then opened the books he was selling and I read according to the laws of nature there exists time and cycles for opposing forces to rule. The example used was death and life and how they both exist by where one is the other is not because of the cycles of nature. With that alone I bought 3 books from the guy and headed back up to Yonkers. I remember driving up the Henry Hudson when things were said to me on that subject of the universal law, eventually happening in my life. I learned from experience that I can't prepare for it because I don't know where or when it's going to happen. I have no control over its' divine timing.

So, I'm back at the office trying to reach deadlines. I have videos to schedule, shows to book, and albums are due. It's time to feed the dogs, and I get a call from Rowdy City, and he says Superior you will never believe what I'm about to tell you. What is that? He said that we have a show in Connecticut and you will never guess who we are opening for. Who? He said DMX.

Immediately my life starts to flash in front of me everything is spinning and he's calling my name on the other side of the phone asking me if I am alright. To him this was a real major step in his career and development. He is excited and as for the rest of the kennel they always wanted me to introduce them to X.

Meanwhile I'm thinking about the last time I spoke with X. I got on the phone and the last two words he said to me was **Fuck you** and he hung up the phone. I get a call from Grease asking me about some music and there was no love there either. The last words we had with one another over the phone it ended up on a sour note. I don't know what to expect when I finally see him again; it could be peace or it could be war depending on if he is high or drunk, and who's in his head that day.

I was like I don't think some of my team is going to be much help for me I have to bring in reinforcements to protect myself. These people don't know how Ruff Ryders roll. Plus DMX can really get on some bullshit sometimes. I really didn't know what to expect. All of this is running through my head as he is talking to me about the date and the show. The rest of the team is excited because they are about to do a show and open for DMX. I was like cool let me finish my business and we will talk tomorrow. When I got off the phone all I was thinking about was it was about to go down and I had to get ready. My team got stars in their eyes but if things go ugly, some of us will get hit across the head and they will also see some stars, literally.

For the next couple of weeks I went through several emotions in anticipation of the day. That day me and X will be in the same building, and the only good thing about it is that I have a heads up on knowing he is going to be there and him not knowing my connection to the group opening up. He didn't have the slightest clue about my appearance and my connection to Rowdy City, the group that's going to open for him.

The day of the show everyone is excited. For years my people were privileged to listen to exclusive rare DMX footage that I have in the archives and everyone was aware of my history with X. The recent documentary that I participated in with VH1 for DMX behind the music has my label buzzing. I thought about it and said to myself if I didn't know DMX and all of his bullshit, I would probably be happy to meet him also. But the nigga did me dirty so fuck him. I don't think we will ever have what we once had or even live out the plans we envisioned back in the projects. I'm still trying to figure out why he cut me off as soon as he got on. He made some money, had new friends, and a new team where many of those new people capitalized from X and most never did any real work.

(Exploitation) For that Reason alone I am looking for the chance to go across his head. It kills me to listen to him talk about his dogs and how he takes care of them. It's all bullshit, that's all TV and music, but it does sound good.

The day came we are in Connecticut and it was Show Time. As we went into the venue I was saying to myself that I was one of the most important figures in the building. I gave the world DMX and now my new group is opening for him. Everything is now coming full circle 360 degrees. Is this what my grandmother was talking about when she was teaching about the law of karma?

As soon as we get into the building it was time for us to hit the stage and we did what we do best. We ripped the mic and put our work in. When it was all said and done, we got much love from the crowd. When the show was over we went back in to the VIP room and as were on the way there I thought we was going to run into X so I was preparing for the real show be he wasn't there yet. I see that he was still on his Hollywood.

As time was going by, anxiety was building up in anticipation of his arrival. All of a sudden I hear the crowd escalating and DJ saying DMX is in the building. Now I am like damn it's about to go down as I look around, and see my soldiers caught up in the moment. They weren't really aware of what was really about to go down. I see a few dudes from his camp come into the VIP. So I play the corner in the cut and begin to clutch my sweaty palm reflecting back on my experiences with X, I know you got to get him first and make it count because if not he is going to shed some blood to the white meat.

Now, I'm looking at a few dudes in his camp acting all cocky not realizing that they would have a job if it weren't for the work that I put in. They're acting like monkeys. I'm just laughing at them saying those are DMX new yes men AKA Male groupies. Then out of nowhere X walks through the doors and he came in and looked at me and I was like oh shit!

Then, he looked away and took a double take and said Superior is that Superior? Then he came up to me, I didn't know what to expect because he can be smiling then the next minute knock you the fuck out. As he was approaching me I was moving in slow motion and the closer he got I clutched my fist. Then, to my surprise he gave me a hug and some dap. He was telling everyone that's my man it was just me and him in the beginning. I was like Oh shit as I released my tightly closed fist and embraced him with love in return. As I'm hugging the brother, I'm thinking about is this what my grandma was talking about when she was teaching the law of Karma; because the situation with me and X came full circle from Mulford gardens in the beginning, to many years later in Connecticut. I was happy that the rest of the pups got a chance to see the "grand champ".

Finally, it was show time and X hit the stage with lots of energy and feeding from the energy of the crowd. Everyone that knows or has been to concerts with X, know that he has one of the best stage presence that hip hop has to offer. I was told to come up on the stage and I just played the corner and was just watching. Saying the lyrics in my mind thinking about all the ups and downs we had together and what we had been through. Having flash backs of the freestyle sessions in my room, developing and building formula for success. Then I held up my head high and said this is what I helped to create. This came from my hard work, blood, sweat and tears. Then I snapped out of it and enjoyed the rest of the show.

SUPERIOR & DMX

DMX PERFORMS AT LAST SHOW PRIOR TO ARREST INOCTOBER 2010 CONNECTICUT

But just like in the past things were going too smooth and for X that doesn't last too long. X had the crowd rocking and he was in his zone, but the owners of the club said it was time to wrap it up and X wasn't trying to hear that. So next, they cut off the power to the system which included to the mic. That's when X went off! He started screaming and yelling...cussing and he picked up an empty bottle of Hennessey and was about to throw it at the people who cut the system off. I was like, this nigga is still crazy. Nothing changed about him.

Now, the crowd is really going bananas, escalating, and X is screaming. It got so bad they had to get him out of the building and a couple of days later I hear he is in jail again. It was just like Deja-vu as though I've seen this all before. What you see is what you get. As for the future of DMX when he gets out of jail? He will still rise to the top. The real question is will he ever come clean with D.J. Superior "my manz and them."

Regardless of what happens I must still give the world the opportunity to hear the unreleased priceless footage that hip hop fans have been longing for; because America and the worldalways cheers for the underdog.

NEWS

DMX Released From Prison Today

Tuesday, July 19, 2011 11:25 AM | 70 comments
By Champtown and Grandmaster Grouchy Greg

(AllHipHop News) Rap star DMX is officially a free man, as the rapper was released from prison in Yuma, Arizona today (July 19th).

The rapper was greeted by a small group of friends and family upon his release today.

Sources close to DMX told AllHipHop.com that his first stop would be a visit to his probation officer, followed by a shopping trip.

Then, DMX is slated to take up residency in an unknown area of the state.

"I spoke to my daughter, I just got off the phone with my wife," DMX told AllHipHop.com in an exclusive interview. "I'm going to go see my daughter while the sun is up then I'm going to be in the studio man."

DMX, born Earl Simmons, was originally sentenced to one year in prison in December of 2010, after he violated his probation by refusing to submit to a drug test and other minor infractions.

He served seven months of the prison sentence, after being given credit for the 100 days he spent incarcerated awaiting trial.

"Our goal is to keep DMX on the right track, and get him back to work," a member of DMX's inner circle told AllHipHop.com.

According to sources, DMX is currently lining up a number of shows and fielding offers for television, movie and recording projects.

Reps for DMX confirmed that he was in serious negotiations with Rick Ross' Maybach Music Group, although an official offer has yet to be made.

DMX is being managed/booked by Carl "Blacksmif" Smith.

ABOUT THE AUTHOR

Jerome "Raw Rome" Enders grew up in the Housing Projects called Mulford Gardens in Yonkers, N.Y. He was influenced by the rich hip-hop culture of the town, and eventually evolved as a lyricist, poet, and now author. He was accredited for helping to set the foundation in the rich Yonkers hip-hop culture.

Refer to The Lox Wikipedia where it states: **While the local rap scene was being dominated by artists like Raw Rome, Lord Devon and a young DMX**.

Raw Rome was also featured on Styles P Freshman album "Gangster and a Gentleman."

Jerome is currently positioning himself as a highly sought after ghost writer, screen writer, and author's author.

For more information go to www.jeromeenders.com.

AUTHOR'S LAST WORDS

Thanks to the Most High, family and friends for the support in keeping me strong. Thanks to everyone who supported Yonkers the Lost City of Hip-Hop, and making it possible to release my second book. Thanks to my Georgia family for the support… the Down South love is real.

Thanks to Attorney Roy Miller (Atlanta/Macon) for his time and expertise. Thanks to Dr.Larmia Robbins-Brinson PH.D for educating me on mental health and contributing to the project; also thank you to Dr. Brian Reese for coming through when I needed him.

Dr. York, thank you for teaching me the science of books.

And to Scribe Freelance Book Design Company for the interior conversion and publishing advice.

I cannot forget to thank Nabt Ankh Sent Nut (Yvette) for giving 110%! Much love…

Shout out to:

- Chi-Chi Maloni up-coming fashion trend designer
- Tokyo Drift'n A.K.A Magic Hands hair dresser for the trend setters.
- Bea Montgomery of Bea's Mothership Connection and Marketing Media N.Y, N.Y.- mothership3000@msn.com.
- Don Ghotti Brand Innovator & Social Media Expert.
- Of Course the one and only Petey Staxx.
- Zoser Research & Development Institute of Human Relations.
- Abi YahYah (r.i.p.).
- Steve Streets of Scribes & Vibes Atlanta-Conyers, GA.
- Marilyn Neal from All about Books, ATL.
- Peace to Brother John (Tashera's father).
- Terry Clark A.K.A. Mr. Computer Head.
- To the Imperial Jaycee from the Herculoids one of the original founding fathers of hip-hop much success to your radio station www.flex103.1.com.

- Much respect to Les love, Kendo, Black Cannon and the rest of Harlem Lanes radio for always showing love.
- Mary J. Blige for opening up the door and leading the way.
- Lauryn Hill "Everything is Everything."
- DMX for taking what we have in Yonkers and giving it to the world. If it wasn't for you this book wouldn't be possible!
- Last but not least Mom Dukes & Fe-Fe for holding me down!!

D.J. SUPERIOR'S LAST WORDS

A special thanks to Wednesday A.K.A. Clark Kent for being my right hand man and putting in years of work.

Much respect to Styles P and D-Block for being easy to talk to and have a conversation with.

Shout out to:
Paul Dent Co-Executive Producer "Straight out of Yonkers" project.